Concepts in cladding

General Editor: Colin Bassett, BSc, FCIOB, FFB

Cladding of Buildings, A.J. Brookes
The Technology of Suspended Cable Net Structures, F.M. Chaplin, G. Calderbank and J.F. Howes

Related titles
Joints in Buildings, B. Martin (George Godwin)

4

Concepts
in cladding

Case studies of jointing
for architects and engineers

Alan Brookes

Construction Press
London and New York

Construction Press
an imprint of:

Longman Group Limited
Longman House, Burnt Mill, Harlow
Essex CM20 2JE, England
Associated companies throughout the world

Published in the United States of America
by Longman Inc., New York

First published 1985

British Library Cataloguing in Publication Data
Brookes, Alan
   Concepts in cladding: case studies of jointing
     for architects and engineers.
   1. Building materials
   I. Title
   693   TA403

ISBN 0-86095-902-3

Library of Congress Cataloging in Publication Data
Brookes, Alan, 1939–
   Concepts in cladding.

   Bibliography: p.
   Includes index.
   1. Building — Details.   2. Architecture — Details.
I. Title.
TH2025.B76 1985   698   84–29294
ISBN 0–86095–902–3

Set in 10/12pt Linotron Plantin
Printed and Bound in Great Britain
at the Bath Press, Avon

Contents

Acknowledgements   vi

Introduction   vii

 1 Aztec West (units 1400 and 1600), Bristol   1

 2 Bespak Factory, King's Lynn, Norfolk   8

 3 Burne House Telecommunications Centre, London   12

 4 Bush Lane House, London   16

 5 Civic Centre, Chester-le-Street, County Durham   20

 6 Colonnades Garden Centre, London   25

 7 Danish Embassy, Sloane Street, London   29

 8 The Festival Hall, Liverpool   32

 9 Fleetguard Factory, Quimper, Brittany, France   37

10 Greene King Brewery, Draught Beer Plant, Bury
    St Edmunds, Suffolk   41

11 Herman Miller Factory, Bath   47

12 Herman Miller Warehouse, Chippenham, near Bath   51

13 Hochhaus Dresdner Bank AG, Frankfurt/Main, Germany   56

14 IBM Midlands Marketing Centre, Warwick   61

15 IBM Sports Hall, Hursley Park, Winchester   64

16 INMOS Microchip Factory, Newport, Gwent   69

17 Lloyd's Redevelopment, London   75

18 Milton Keynes Advanced Factory Units, Kiln Farm,
    Milton Keynes   81

19 Norweb Offices, Ashton-under-Lyne   87

20 Patera System Building, Stoke-on-Trent   90

21 Renault Centre, Swindon, Wilts   100

22 Sainsbury Centre for the Visual Arts, Norwich   114

23 Schreiber House, Chester   120

24 Schreiber Furniture Factory, Runcorn   124

25 South Poplar Health Centre, London   127

26 Thames Water Authority, New Operations and
    Visitors' Centre, Fobney   131

27 UOP Fragrances Factory, Tadworth, Surrey   137

28 Water Research Centre, Swindon   140

29 Willis Faber and Dumas Insurance Building, Ipswich   144

30 Winwick Quay 4 and 7, Industrial Units, Warrington   148

Index   155

Acknowledgements

Teachers of building construction will know of the frustration of seeing students whose design intentions outstrip their knowledge of relevant technology and who, so often, accept a compromise in the integrity of their design by producing inappropriate technical back-up. Similarly, it is embarrassing when architects in practice misapply detailing because of lack of available knowledge on available materials and methods of construction. In an attempt to give advice on current practice, as part of my teaching in the fourth year at the Liverpool School of Architecture, I had assembled a series of case studies of some recent well-known buildings, which are now collated here in book form.

I am indebted to so many of my students for their co-operation in releasing drawings and photographs from their portfolios, which support the case studies. Also, I would like to thank my colleagues, Steve Haughton and Dave King, for their help and encouragement during the time of preparing the manuscript.

I am grateful for all the helpful advice and contributions from the many architectural practices, whose work is included here, and to the manufacturers who have contributed to the study; these would include Ron Howarth from Climax Gaskets, Les Ratcliffe from Modern Art Glass and Don Reynolds for their advice on glazing techniques, Nigel Dale for his contribution on the Patera System, Mr McLoughlin of Crawford Doors and Hans Siedentopf of Josef Gartner for supplying photographs, Frank Holliday for his explanation of Superplastic aluminium and to Richard Irving of RVP Building Products for assisting my wider understanding of metalforming techniques.

Additional artwork was prepared by Chris Grech and Tony Flannery, and my thanks for the typing go to Vera Doud and Catherine Sutton for all the late-night stints on the word processor.

Finally, my thanks to my family, Jackie, Nicholas, Sarah and James, for their support during the time of preparing the manuscript.

Introduction

It has always been necessary, in order to cope with a sudden expansion in a building programme, to develop standard solutions for constructing buildings. The standard doors and window casements for Georgian houses, the UK industrialised building programme for houses and schools of the 1960s or the present Soviet building programme for mass housing, using precast concrete panels, all come to mind as examples of the industry rationalising its building techniques.

Gradually, using standard techniques, architects develop a body of experience, which enables the designers of assemblies to anticipate the kinds of constructional method available and for the type of materials selected to relate to known patterns of behaviour in use. Often the application of standard techniques also reflects a general acceptance of common cultural objectives within the profession. This ability to learn from experience and from each other is, of course, the major benefit of developing building systems. The disadvantage is that such standard solutions can become monotonous and may even fail to take account of innovations in new materials or changes in use.

In Britain, during the last decade, there has been a move away from industrialised building methods, the myths of mass production have been exposed (see Russell[4]) and the public has become disenchanted with the results of the building systems notion. Architects are turning, more and more, to the use of new materials and innovative techniques often in advance of the technology available to them. Jan Kaplicky and David Nixon with their future systems (Fig. 0.1) would be an example of this pioneering attitude towards building design. The themes developed by Jean Prouvé during the 1930s are being realised and components such as semi-monocoque steel panels are now a practical solution to a building envelope[3].

A new force in architecture, characterised by Foster Associates, Richard Rogers and Partners and Michael Hopkins Architects, has used the idea of surveying a market, analysing the need and integrating this with new and developing technologies. Reporting in the *New Scientist*, 11

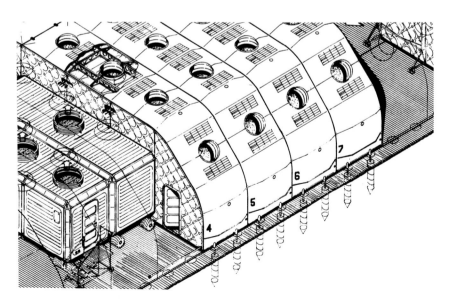

Fig. 0.1 Semi-monocoque steel panel assembly (Courtesy of Jan Kaplicky)

December 1980, Ted Stevens[5] describes 'the new breed of architectural practice which has brought a breath of fresh air to the profession. The new firms specialise in new materials and techniques sometimes borrowing technical ideas from industries that have nothing to do with building – cars, aerospace and plastics for instance.'

In the *Architectural Review* of the development of 'High Tech', Buchanan[2] argues that such an approach 'extends an intermittent British tradition of introducing rationalised industrial technology into building construction'. Some might also claim that, although 'High Tech' pretends to be concerned with larger issues of process, it is more concerned with creating stunning individual buildings (with buildings as objects) than with more general patterns of architecture and urbanism.

Whatever the truth, it cannot be denied that in this country during the last decade the result of this approach to architecture has been to produce some highly individual designs, incorporating many innovations in their constructional details. The danger is that although many of these buildings represent the best of this new style they have many imitators, who may not always be aware of some of the background to the development of the details and may be tempted to use them out of context.

One difficulty may be that, whereas standard textbooks are available for the more traditional forms of construction, for 'High Tech' there is no standard body of information whereby designers can compare the performance of the new products and their assembly. Architects and architectural students rely on the architectural magazines for the source material of these newer forms of construction, many of which give conflicting information or lack of specific details on fixing and jointing. Furthermore, it is not always possible to examine the buildings at first hand. Many of the projects illustrated are located in the country and are not always open to visitors without prior appointment. Although it is possible to walk around and examine the cladding at Herman Miller factory in Bath (see case study 11), it is almost impossible to visit the INMOS building (case study 16) due to the sensitive nature of its contents.

In order to provide architects and architectural students with a reference source of this type of construction, I have collected these thirty case studies of what are, essentially, very individual approaches to detailing, mainly in British buildings constructed between 1973 and 1983. The further reading list is intended to direct those students or architects wishing to know more about the particular building of interest to source material in the architectural press. The reader should also be aware that many of these details have evolved after intensive dialogue between architects and manufacturers. A characteristic of this new age of design is that the leading architectural firms are willing to negotiate with manufacturers over products designed specifically for larger building projects. The development of performance specifications over the 1960s greatly assisted in presenting a basis for this dialogue to take place.

The details mainly show cladding assemblies, for that is the primary purpose of this book. However, where possible, the related form of structure has also been described for it is the spanning characteristics of any given material that determines the form of construction. Many of the details include gasket jointing, either in neoprene, EPDM or silicone. The development of neoprene gaskets took place in the early 1960s led by manufacturers such as Redfern Rubber and later by Leyland and Birmingham Rubber Company. Figure 0.2 shows a comparison of gasket size used in some of the buildings included here. One might reflect that this form of jointing, so characteristic of 'High Tech' design, would not be available but for the Consortia School Building Programme (mainly CLASP) who persuaded the rubber manufacturers, at that time involved in the automobile industry, to invest in the development of gaskets for building. Usually, these gaskets are expressed as a grid on the outside face of the building.

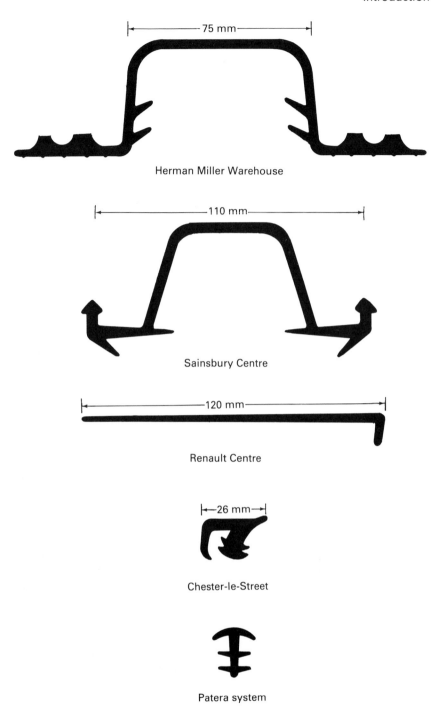

Fig. 0.2 Comparison of neoprene gasket sizes used in the case studies

Waschmann[6] reminds us, in his concept of the universal joint, that:

> The joint is not a necessary evil. Accordingly, it does not need to be concealed with seal strips and so on like an object of shame. It stands out as a formative element which has evolved with progress in technology ... these joints not only indicate zones of contact but scrupulously define any object they enclose. They not only reflect processes of aesthetic importance but represent the results of technical functions and are to be understood as such. Their place is determined by materials and methods, structural principles, standards and modular order, i.e. ... In the perfect relationship of object, function and separation, the joint communicates a new visual attitude.

Another factor affecting many of the details was the continual search for an interchangeable assembly of factory-made components influenced mainly by Charles Eames' own house (1949) and the development of the Californian SCSD School systems, led by Ezra Ehrenkrantz, in which components could be rearranged to suit a particular client need. You will note the continual theme of interchangeable quick assembly methods linking many of the case studies included here.

The big question mark still remaining over all these details relates to their long-term performance in use. Whereas in other industries the designer has the opportunity to carry out trials, tests and modifications before the final product is declared satisfactory, in the building industry each product is, in fact, a prototype until sufficient numbers of examples have been tried and tested over a period of time. Many of the factors affecting the long-term performance of the assemblies illustrated are still unknown. For example, the effects of ageing on exposed neoprene and silicone gaskets are still subject to speculation. The problems of delamination of composite panel construction, due to thermal bowing, is still a relatively new science, and pre-coated sheet materials used in many of the examples quoted are subject to a different life to first maintenance, according to their colour or even position on the building envelope.

Although students, when challenged on the practicality of their proposals, often claim that 'it must work because it has been used before', in the true sense of engineering science, these new solutions cannot be said to be 'tried and tested' even though they might appear to be working perfectly satisfactorily at the moment. The reader should not therefore assume that the inclusion of a particular detail in this book necessarily endorses its use.

What is emerging is a change of attitude towards design responsibility and an apparent desire to innovate and experiment. Strangely, clients appear to encourage this, perhaps anxious to promote the idea of a progressive corporate image through their building and choice of architect. This is not an entirely new phenomenon as, after all, Brunelleschi was sponsored by the Medici for the same reason. Perhaps what is new are the changes of roles within the professions. In many 'High Tech' buildings, engineers take on greater responsibility for what was previously thought to be the province of the architect. Manufacturers are increasingly being asked to produce new designs in conjunction with architects, leading sometimes to conflicts over rights of patent. Where these new relationships are formed carefully, the solutions arising from co-operation between designers and manufacturers can be spectacular. As has previously been suggested, it is the application of these results to a wider sphere that can sometimes cause concern.

Thus, the information contained within is intended as no more than a contribution towards a greater understanding of the constructional method achieved in these thirty examples illustrating the state of the art. I do not intend to validate these proposals or even to justify their use. The details are shown hoping that all those involved in the building process will improve their vocabulary of detailing in lightweight construction and be more aware of the factors involved in their application in practice.

Further reading

1. Ackermann, K. (1984)
   'Industriebau' Deutsche Verlags-Anstalt, Stuttgart 1984

2. Buchanan, P (1983)
   'High Tech – another British thoroughbred', *Architectural Review*, July 1983, 15–19

3. Nixon, D & Kaplicky, J (1983)
   'Skin', *Architectural Review* (High-tech Issue), July 1983, 54–9

4. Russell, B (1981)
   Building systems, Industrialisation and Architecture. Wiley, London 1981

5. Stevens, T (1980)
   'Putting the tech into architecture', *New Scientist*, 11 Dec. 1980, 704–5

6. Waschmann, K (1961)
   The Turning Point of Buildings: Structure and Design. Reinhold Publishing, New York, 1961

Case Study 1   Aztec West (units 1400 and 1600), Bristol

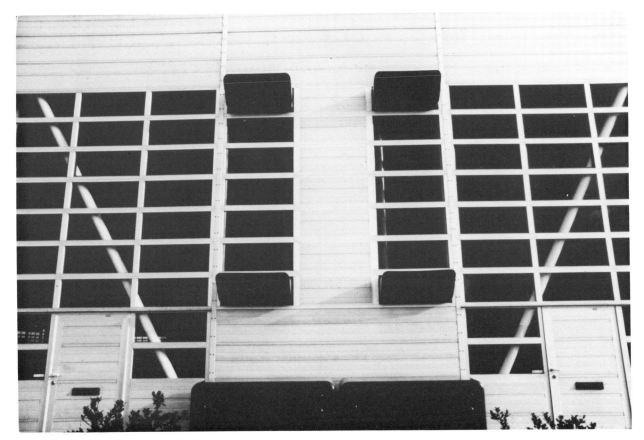

Fig. 1.1 General view of units 1400 and 1600 showing aluzinc steel cladding panels by Crawford Door Ltd (Courtesy of Crawford Door Ltd)

General

Eight miles north-west of Bristol and near to the intersection of the M4 from London to Wales and the M5 from the south-west of England to the Midlands, lies the new industrial park and business community of Aztec West. With its shiny, High-Tech buildings and landscaped parkland, Aztec West is reminiscent of American style industrial parks of the Silicon Valley variety.

The first two buildings built in the park, by architects Nicholas Grimshaw and Partners, consist of a speculative mixed-use development and are an identical pair (referred to as 1400 and 1600) differentiated only by the colour of their jointing gaskets and bollards: in one case red and the other blue, set against their overall silver colour. They face each other across a parking and services court. Each is almost square in plan, 8350 m² in area and designed to subdivide into units, size varying from 800 m².

Once again, following the traditions of the Herman Miller Factory in Bath and Winwick Quay 4 (see separate case studies 11 and 30), Nicholas Grimshaw designed an interchangeable facade which would respond to an unknown client's requirements for doors, glazing and services.

The deflection drained structure was similar to that used at Winwick

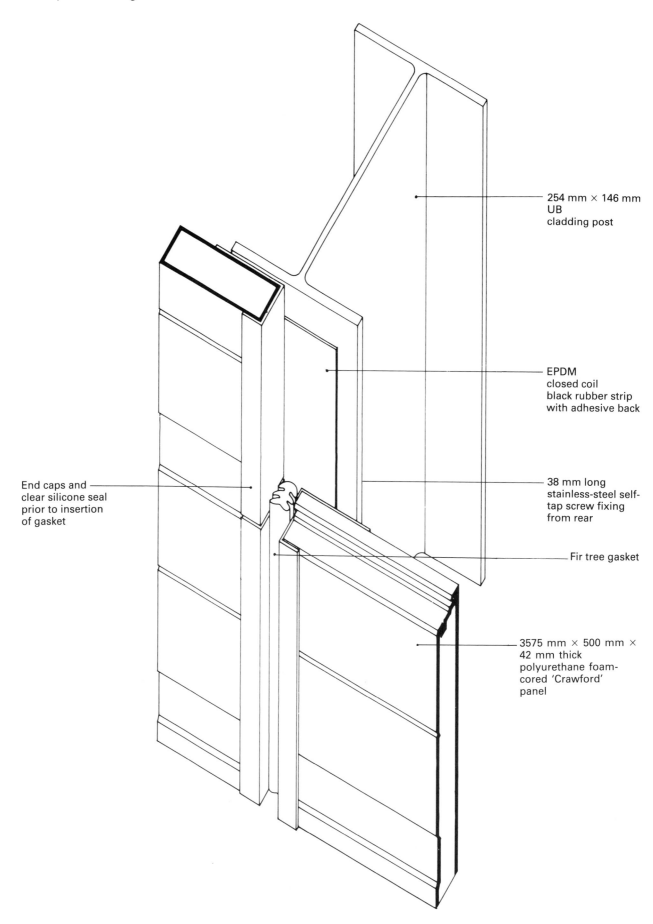

254 mm × 146 mm
UB
cladding post

EPDM
closed coil
black rubber strip
with adhesive back

End caps and
clear silicone seal
prior to insertion
of gasket

38 mm long
stainless-steel self-
tap screw fixing
from rear

Fir tree gasket

3575 mm × 500 mm ×
42 mm thick
polyurethane foam-
cored 'Crawford'
panel

Fig. 1.2 Units 1400 and 1600. Panel to panel mounted on steel subframe, as designed
(Courtesy of Clive Gray)

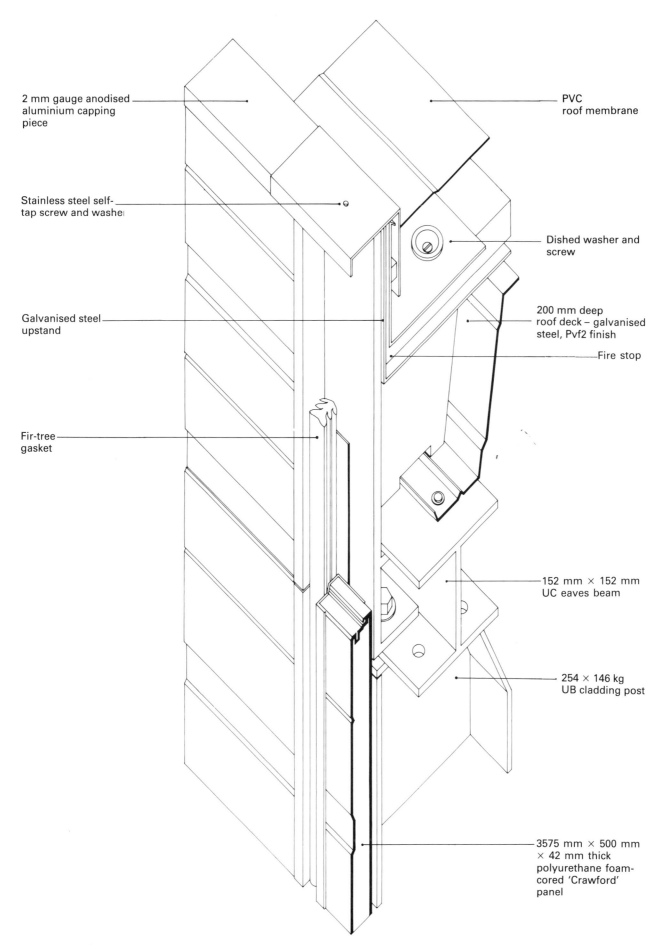

2 mm gauge anodised aluminium capping piece

PVC roof membrane

Stainless steel self-tap screw and washer

Dished washer and screw

200 mm deep roof deck – galvanised steel, Pvf2 finish

Galvanised steel upstand

Fire stop

Fir-tree gasket

152 mm × 152 mm UC eaves beam

254 × 146 kg UB cladding post

3575 mm × 500 mm × 42 mm thick polyurethane foam-cored 'Crawford' panel

Fig. 1.3 Units 1400 and 1600. Roof eaves to panel detail, as designed

Quay 4. Pioneered by engineer Peter Brett, this was constructed using Plannja deep-profile metal decking spanning 10.8 m within a structural grid of 18.6 m by 10.8 m and 7.2 m clear height to the underside of the beams. The lattice beams, made up from rectangular hollow sections, are designed as simply supported spans to avoid bottom-chord compression at the columns. Horizontal bracings between beams are provided to counter wind forces.

Cladding

The silver-coloured aluzinc steel cladding panels by Crawford Door Limited consist of their '342 system' panel mounted on the steel subframe structure. These panels, originally developed for up and over garage doors, consist of two sheets of steel with polyurethane foam insulation core (total thickness 42 mm).

The original joint, using coloured fir-cone-shaped gaskets, did not perform satisfactorily, due to a larger joint size than anticipated. Joints were re-sealed on site and aluminium cover strip has now been fixed over the vertical joints. Fixing is carried out from inside with the fixings screwed into reinforcing bands at the top and bottom of each panel.

Benson Electrics

Another building of interest on the same site, by architects Brian Taggart Associates for Benson Electrics, uses cladding in a loosely composed chequer board of interchangeable double-glazed opening units and vacuum-formed sandwich panels, each 1.0 m by 1.8 m. These panels were manufactured by Superform Metals Limited, Worcester, using super-plastic aluminium 'Supral 5000' alloy, developed from the material used by Foster

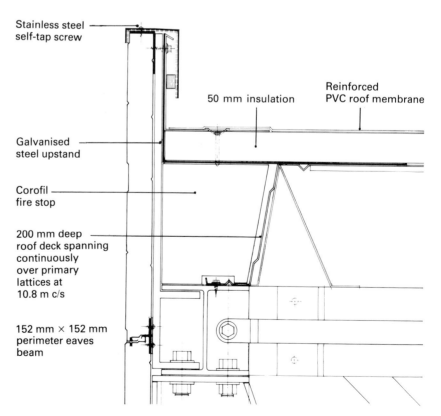

Fig. 1.4 Units 1400 and 1600. Section through roof/panel detail

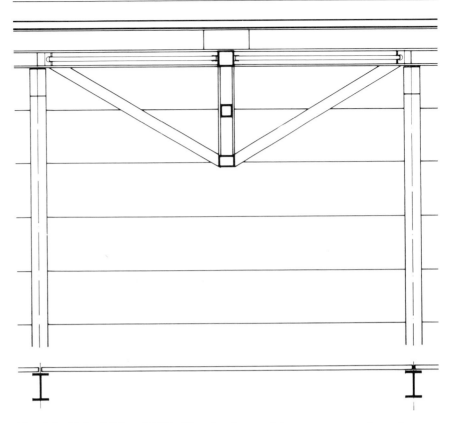

Fig. 1.5 Units 1400 and 1600. Plan showing modular arrangement of panels

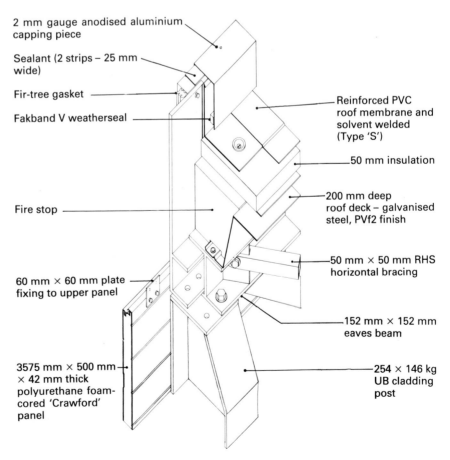

2 mm gauge anodised aluminium capping piece

Sealant (2 strips – 25 mm wide)

Fir-tree gasket

Fakband V weatherseal

Reinforced PVC roof membrane and solvent welded (Type 'S')

50 mm insulation

Fire stop

200 mm deep roof deck – galvanised steel, PVf2 finish

50 mm × 50 mm RHS horizontal bracing

60 mm × 60 mm plate fixing to upper panel

152 mm × 152 mm eaves beam

3575 mm × 500 mm × 42 mm thick polyurethane foam-cored 'Crawford' panel

254 × 146 kg UB cladding post

Fig. 1.6 Units 1400 and 1600. Panel assembly at eaves showing fixings

Fig. 1.7 Cover pieces for jointing on units 1400 and 1600

Fig. 1.8 General view of Benson Electrics under construction. Architects: Brian
Taggart Associates

Fig. 1.9 Installation of Supral 5000 panels at Benson Electrics (Courtesy of Superform Metals Ltd)

Associates for the Sainsbury Centre (see case study 22). The panels have a polyester powder coat finish and have a 40 mm layer of 'styrofoam' bonded to the inner face. The cladding panels are incorporated into a frame and panel system by Essex Aluminium, Southminster.

Further reading

1. Buchanan, P (1983)
   'Business Park Bristol', *Architectural Review*, Nov. 1983, 38–45

2. British Steel Corporation (1982)
   Aztec West Development, S H S Project File 1, British Steel Corporation Tubes Division: Ref. TD 272/10E/82

3. Morton-Smith, G, Taggart, B. & Burns, J (1982)
   'A new setting for British industry', *Chartered Quantity Surveyor*, Sept. 1982

Case Study 2   Bespak Factory, King's Lynn, Norfolk

Fig. 2.1 Overall view of Bespak Factory

General

This factory, making plastic valves for aerosol bottles and cans, is situated on the North Lynn Industrial Estate, King's Lynn, Norfolk. Designed by Cambridge Design and built in 1979, the building is an extension to an existing factory and includes both production space and offices.

Structure

220 mm diameter circular section steel columns on a grid 13.5 m square support the unusual 'umbrella-like' roof structure consisting of four trusses composed of 168 mm circular hollow steel sections spanning across the diagonals of the square bay connected by 36 mm diameter tie rods. Secondary trusses connect the apex of each bay to the next. The circular columns also contain the rain water downpipes, made in one length.

The exposed structure was site painted with bright yellow chlorinated rubber coating.

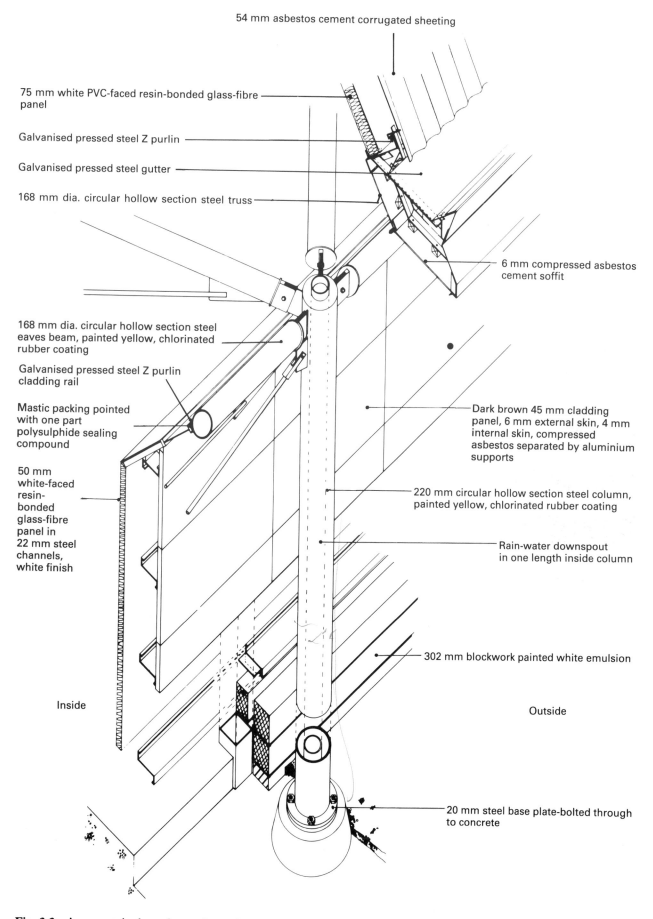

54 mm asbestos cement corrugated sheeting

75 mm white PVC-faced resin-bonded glass-fibre panel

Galvanised pressed steel Z purlin

Galvanised pressed steel gutter

168 mm dia. circular hollow section steel truss

168 mm dia. circular hollow section steel eaves beam, painted yellow, chlorinated rubber coating

Galvanised pressed steel Z purlin cladding rail

Mastic packing pointed with one part polysulphide sealing compound

50 mm white-faced resin-bonded glass-fibre panel in 22 mm steel channels, white finish

Inside

6 mm compressed asbestos cement soffit

Dark brown 45 mm cladding panel, 6 mm external skin, 4 mm internal skin, compressed asbestos separated by aluminium supports

220 mm circular hollow section steel column, painted yellow, chlorinated rubber coating

Rain-water downspout in one length inside column

302 mm blockwork painted white emulsion

Outside

20 mm steel base plate-bolted through to concrete

Fig. 2.2 Axonometric through exterior wall (Courtesy of Marlene Kinrade)

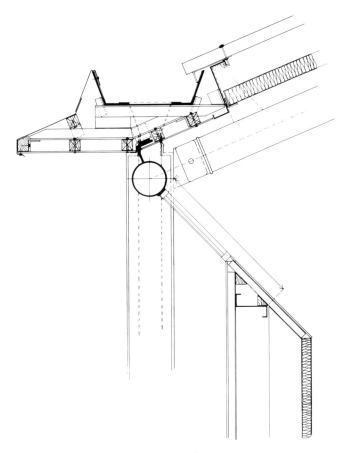

Fig. 2.3 Section at perimeter roof gutter

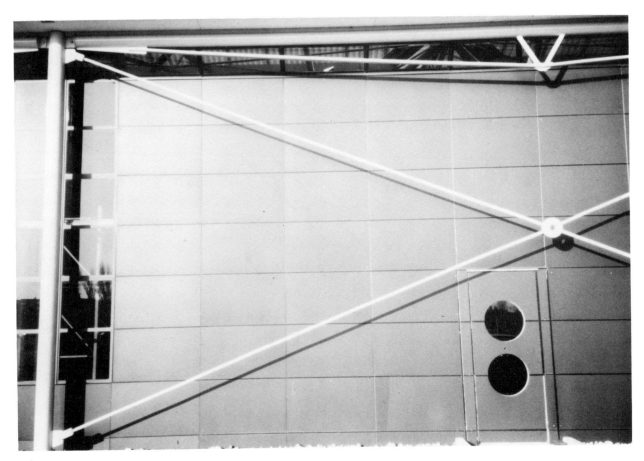

Fig. 2.4 Close-up of one bay with cross bracing

Cladding

The cladding consists of 6 mm 'Eternit' asbestos dark brown outer skin with 4 mm fibre-board lining separated by aluminium supports (total thickness 45 mm) all mounted on cladding rails with a high-level window at 45° tangent to the structural grid. Behind each perimeter column, the cladding is replaced by a vertical strip of glazing.

The roofing was composed of 'big six' asbestos cement outer corrugated sheeting, colour green, with a 75 mm PVC-faced resin-bonded glass-fibre panel, used as an inner lining.

The total cost per m^2 of floor area was £200.00, with the cost of the asbestos cladding panels as £65.25/m^2.

Further reading

1. Cunliffe, R (1980)
   'Building study — factory extension for Bespak Industries', *Architects' Journal*, 2 July 1980, 20–32

Case Study 3   Burne House Telecommunications Centre, London

Fig. 3.1   Overall view of Burne House (Photo by Richard Einzig)

General

This 13-storey high telecommunications centre, standing at the junction of the A40 and Edgware Road, London, is entirely clad in cream-coloured vitreous enamel panels. Designed by Charles Pearson, Son and Partners, in association with the PSA, Directorate of Post Office Services, the building was completed in 1977. Curtain walling was by Crittall Construction Limited with vitreous enamel steel panels supplied by Escol Panels Limited, Wellingborough, Northamptonshire.

Cladding

The cladding module is 3.86 m delineated by the continuous vertical lines of the cleaning cradle guides, with a vertical bay height of 4.42 m, allowing an internal room height of 3.96 m.

Each standard bay of curtain walling consists of fixed and changeable zones. The vertical-fixed zone is 660 mm wide and spans the hollow galvanised steel core mullion, which houses many of the services. The horizontal-fixed zone is 1473 mm deep and spans the concrete floors and upstand walls. Contained within these fixed zones are the changeable areas

Fig. 3.2 Close-up of south-west corner (Photo by Richard Einzig)

3200 mm wide by 2946 mm high, which provide the flexibility of the cladding and can include fixed or openable glazing, louvres for permanent ventilation, louvres as air inlet/outlets and panels of various sizes. The panels with their varying inserts were mounted on to the support framing and sealed in the 'fixed' zones using Adshead Ratcliffe 'Arbokol' 2000 black two-part polysulphide sealant and in the 'changeable' zones using neoprene gaskets, with additional mechanical fixing to satisfy Building Regulations requirements. The panels incorporate insulation board and polyurethane backing.

Although vitreous-enamelled panels are normally restricted in size to 1520 mm maximum width due to the availability of zero carbon flattened steel necessary for their manufacture, in this case, several small panels have been combined into a factory-assembled cladding unit. They were then lifted into place and bolted back against the main structure. The skilful use of large neoprene gaskets at the edge of the panels forming the 'changeable' areas, when contrasted against the smaller factory-sealed polysulphide joints, results in an overall impression of a large-sized panel assembly.

The student of cladding should note this example, in that the subsequent scale of the cladding has not been affected by limitations of manufacturing size, which is often quoted as generating the grid.

13

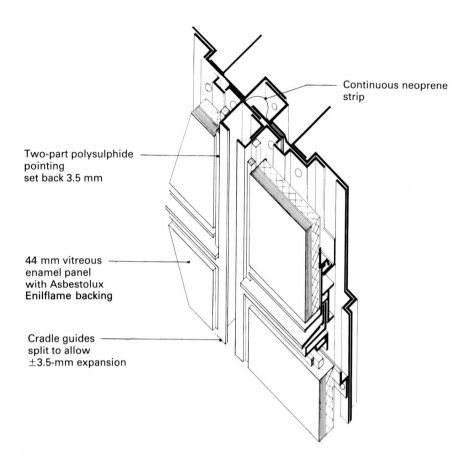

Continuous neoprene strip

Two-part polysulphide pointing set back 3.5 mm

44 mm vitreous enamel panel with Asbestolux Enilflame backing

Cradle guides split to allow ±3.5-mm expansion

Fig. 3.3 Axonometric panel to panel assembly (Courtesy of Keith Rodwell)

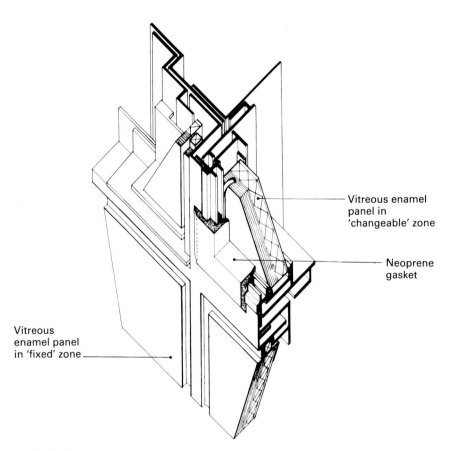

Vitreous enamel panel in 'changeable' zone

Neoprene gasket

Vitreous enamel panel in 'fixed' zone

Fig. 3.4 Axonometric panel to window assembly

14

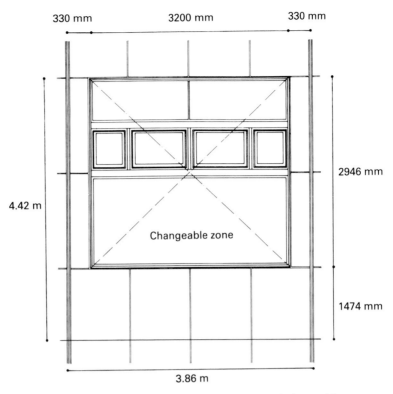

Fig. 3.5   Overall panel dimensions showing fixed and changeable zones

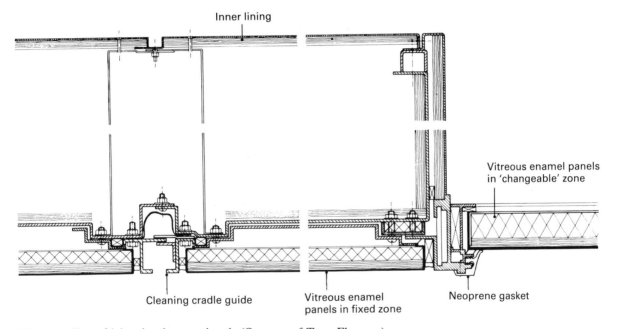

Fig. 3.6   Plan of joint showing panel seals (Courtesy of Tony Flannery)

Further reading

1.   Brookes, A & Ward, M (1981)
     'Sheet metal claddings', *Architects' Journal*, 8 July 1981, 83

2.   Davies, Colin (1977)
     'Fair exchange', *Building*, 6 May 1977

3.   Gale, Adrian (1977)
     'Building Study — Burne House Telecommunications Centre, London', *Architects' Journal*, 16 Feb. 1977, 302–13

Case Study 4 Bush Lane House, London

Fig. 4.1 Overall view of Bush Lane House

General

Bush Lane House, Cannon Street, London, built in 1976, uses a structural lattice of stainless steel, positioned on the outside of the building envelope. These large, hollow tubes of steel are filled with water and, as such, it is the first water-cooled building in Britain. Designed by architects, engineers and quantity surveyors Arup Associates, credit must also go to the Ove Arup Partnership research and development group who convinced the GLC of the feasibility of the design and the use of the novel fire-resistant structure. It is this aspect that often dazzles and fascinates students of architecture and the technical solution to the node connectors, although not strictly related to cladding, is included here for that reason. It must be stressed, however, that this unique and somewhat costly solution to the building envelope arose because of a particular series of circumstances and the possibility of it being used again in the United Kingdom are very remote.

The brief from the client, City and West End Properties Limited, required the provision of the maximum permitted usable floor area within a high-quality lettable city office building. It was also proposed to allow London Transport to construct the tunnel and station to the proposed Fleet Line underground below the site. These conditions were to restrict the location of the foundations to areas not occupied by tunnels and to provide a clear headroom of 10 m from ground level to the underside of the office development. In addition, the height of the building was restricted to 44 m to comply with town planning requirements.

The combination of all these requirements resulted in a somewhat compressed building envelope and the full height lattice framework was positioned outside the building envelope so as not to interrupt the lettable space. This decision then raised a number of issues: corrosion resistance of the steelwork, its cyclic movement due to temperature changes and its fire protection.

Structural fire protection

The adoption of water cooling to fire-protect the steelwork reduced the need for any applied protection as the lattice design with few horizontal members allows the water to flow by natural convection through the structure. The lattice is based on a series of prefabricated frames made up of centrifugally-cast stainless-steel tubes welded to cast nodes. Structural grid is 1.6 m. The frames are of two types: the columns, which weigh up to 13 tonnes and are 9.8 m high by 4.8 m wide; and the lattices, which weigh up to 4 tonnes and are 14.4 m high by 3.2 m wide. The cooling water is contained vertically within each frame width and the side-bolted connections are sealed. The majority of site joints were bolted with high-strength friction-grip bolts at the primary node connections. Site welds occur only at the levels where the

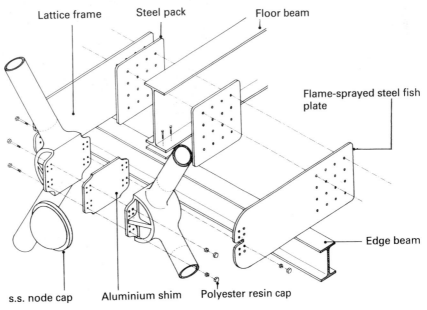

Fig. 4.2 Exploded view of node connection (Courtesy of Mike Rushe)

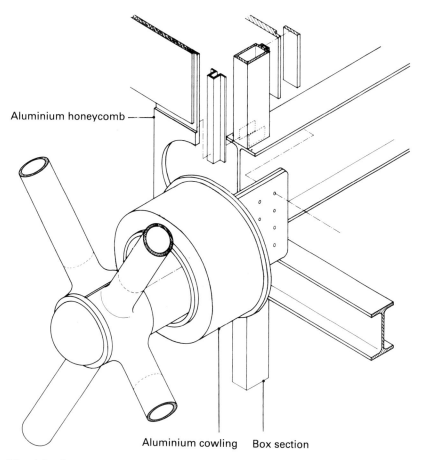

Aluminium honeycomb —

Aluminium cowling   Box section

Fig. 4.3 Axonometric view of node connection

Fig. 4.4 Exposed structural lattice grid (Courtesy of Arup Associates, architects, engineers and quantity surveyors)

frames (the height of which were limited for transportation) fit on top of each other and at the side-to-side connections along the top chord.

Further reading

1. Brandenburger, J, Eatherley, P, & Raines, R (1976)
   'Bush Lane House', *Arup Journal*, Dec. 1976

2. Cooke, G (1974)
   'Technical Study — new methods of fire protection for external steel-work', *Architects' Journal*, 28 Aug. 1974, 511

3. Deeming, N (1983)
   'Fire-safe structural steel', pp 40–52. B. Arch. Dissertation, Liverpool University School of Architecture, 1983

4. Lyall, Sutherland (1980)
   The State of British Architecture. Architectural Press, London, p. 23

5. O'Brien, T (1976)
   'Bush Lane House — water cooling', *Arup Journal*, Dec. 1976, 16

Case Study 5 Civic Centre, Chester-le-Street, County Durham

Fig. 5.1 Overall view of building (Courtesy of Faulkner-Brown Hendy Watkinson Stonor — architects; photo by Richard Bryant)

General

Designed by Faulkner-Brown Hendy Watkinson Stonor and built during 1980–2, this building has been much admired for its sleek, shiny, silver shed form and its distinctive feature of the glazed public mall with its internally-exposed white-painted structure and services.

Structure

The structure of the Chester-le-Street Civic Centre consists of a two-storey steel portal frame facing west, from which five pairs of 21-m long lattice trusses at 7.2-m centres span across amenity and office areas. Above these twin lattices, a triangular-sectioned GRP element creates space for tubular ventilation ducting. The monopitched structure thus formed straddles an existing public footpath by means of the glazed public mall.

Cladding

The external wall consists of an adapted proprietary 'Presslock' curtain-wall glazing system, supporting 'Alucobond' cladding panels. In conjunction with the manufacturers, Modern Art Glass, the architects developed the standard glazing bar (used at Winwick Quay, see case study 30) with both an internal and external glazing flange. A continuous neoprene glazing gasket then fixes both glazed and solid panels to the aluminium framing system. The outer skin, when not glass, consists of a 6-mm aluminium and polyethylene sandwich ('Alucobond'), to which is bonded 40 mm of foil-backed polyurethane insulation (size of panel 2.4 m by 1.2 m). The inner skin is a 6-mm self-finished asbestos cement panel.

The cost of the curtain walling (according to AJ Cost Analysis, 11 August 1982) had a significant element rate of £169.00 per m² for the main elevations and £268.00 per m² for the mall ends, but the deep plan and low perimeter to area ratio helped to reduce the cost impact.

Additional fabrication costs may have been involved in providing the 'stepped' glass/panel joints and chamfered panels at the junction with the angled roof.

The whole wall assembly is effectively hung from the roof, giving a roof to wall detail which does not have to cater for movement. All vertical movement and tolerance are then taken up at the cill by means of a neoprene concertina gasket with wall mullions spigotted to a steel angle fixed to the face of the concrete. A compressible 'compriband' sealing strip then separates the aluminium transoms and the steel angle.

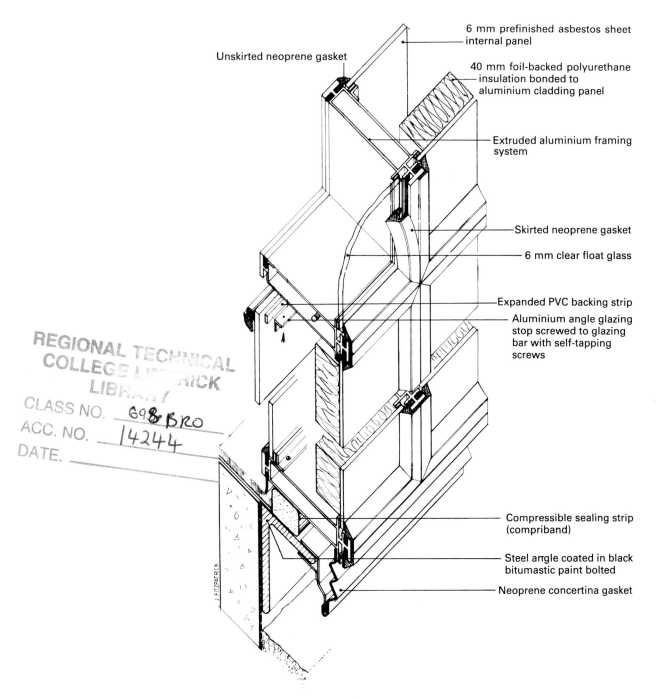

Fig. 5.2 Assembly of 'Alucobond' panels and glazing into the 'Presslock' system (Courtesy of James Fitzpatrick)

21

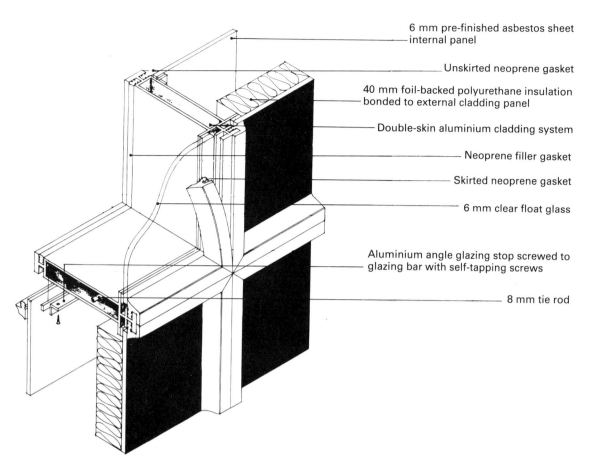

6 mm pre-finished asbestos sheet internal panel

Unskirted neoprene gasket

40 mm foil-backed polyurethane insulation bonded to external cladding panel

Double-skin aluminium cladding system

Neoprene filler gasket

Skirted neoprene gasket

6 mm clear float glass

Aluminium angle glazing stop screwed to glazing bar with self-tapping screws

8 mm tie rod

Fig. 5.3 Cross-over junction showing push-fit neoprene gaskets (Courtesy of Chris Burscough)

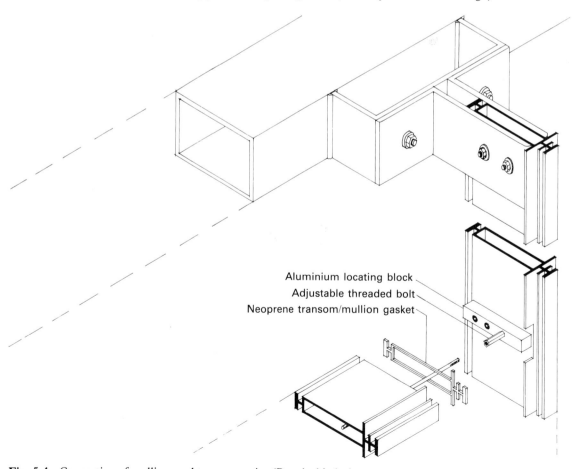

Aluminium locating block
Adjustable threaded bolt
Neoprene transom/mullion gasket

Fig. 5.4 Connection of mullions and transoms using 'Presslock' glazing system

Fig. 5.5 Fixing of neoprene window gaskets (Courtesy of Faulkner-Brown Hendy Watkinson Stonor — architects; photo by Jeremy Preston)

Fig. 5.6 Corner detail of panel showing neoprene concertina gasket at cill level

Further reading

1. Allies, Bob (1983)
   'A R detail No. 2', *Architectural Review*, May 1983

2. Buchanan, Peter (1982)
   'Chester-le-Street Civic Centre, Co. Durham', *Architectural Review*, Aug. 1982, 43–52

3. British Steel Corporation (1982)
   'Chester-le-Street District Council Offices', SHS Project File 4, ref. TD 272/10E/82. British Steel Corporation Tubes Division

4. Faulkner-Brown Hendy Watkinson Stonor (1982)
   'Chester-le-Street Civic Centre, Co. Durham', *Architects' Journal*, 4 Aug. 1982 and 11 Aug. 1982, 31–46

5. Fitzpatrick, J (1982)
   '*Technical Study — Chester-le-Street*', Liverpool University School of Architecture, Oct. 1982

Case Study 6   Colonnades Garden Centre, London

Fig. 6.1   Garden Centre during assembly (Courtesy of Terry Farrell Partnership)

General

Designed in 1980, the Colonnades Garden Centre, at Bishops Bridge Road, Bayswater, London, for Clifton Nurseries, represented a unique application of twin-wall polycarbonate sheeting used in conjunction with a lightweight demountable steel structure. The architects, Terry Farrell Partnership, worked in conjunction with the raw material manufacturers, Bayer (UK) Limited, to develop a system of construction which was the forerunner of the later, more complicated version used at the Liverpool Garden Festival Building (see case study 8).

The general concept was an arcade with a greenhouse on one side and a shop selling plants on the other. The lightweight steel frame, designed as a series of seven ladders, spans 5 m between the perimeter of the building to the arcade. The curvilinear profile of the ladders was an aesthetic consideration but also allows for natural stiffening of the flexible polycarbonate, which was supplied in long lengths 2.1 m wide (maximum format available) by 10.5 m. Some difficulty was experienced in handling the 10-mm thick polycarbonate sheets, due to their extremely light weight.

Sequence of assembly

Once the steel frame, comprising arcade frames, cradles and ladders, was erected, the sheets of polycarbonate were offered up for marking of fixing positions to match those in the steel frame before being taken down and drilled. Care was taken to vacuum the drilling swarf out of the flutes. Alternate panels were drilled and fixed in position by the erection crew, composed of final-year architectural students.

Method of fixing

A fixing button was designed by Bayer's research and development department in Germany, which would be capable of spreading the compressive stress over a 50-mm diameter area around the fixing. In order to prevent permanent deformation to the sheet when tightened, the button has a recess for a neoprene washer and a spacer to prevent over-tightening of the bolt. Allowance is made in the size of fixing hole for thermal expansion and the size of 14-gauge self-tapping screw allows for a 10 per cent tolerance on the thickness of the polycarbonate sheet. The screw is totally sealed and hidden by an integral tolerance fit cap, tapped in place over it. According to the *Architects' Journal* cost analysis of 1 October 1980, the cost of the fixing buttons, including dye and tooling cost, represented almost one-quarter of the cost of the polycarbonate cladding quoted (1980) as £2.68/m^2.

Method of jointing

The joint between the polycarbonate sheeting, which follows the structure's alternative concave and convex curves, was formed using a 2-mm thick polyurethane elastomer rubber gasket extruded as a flat shape and curved to fit between the panels and stuck down to the polycarbonate surface using '3M' double-sided acrylic contact tape.

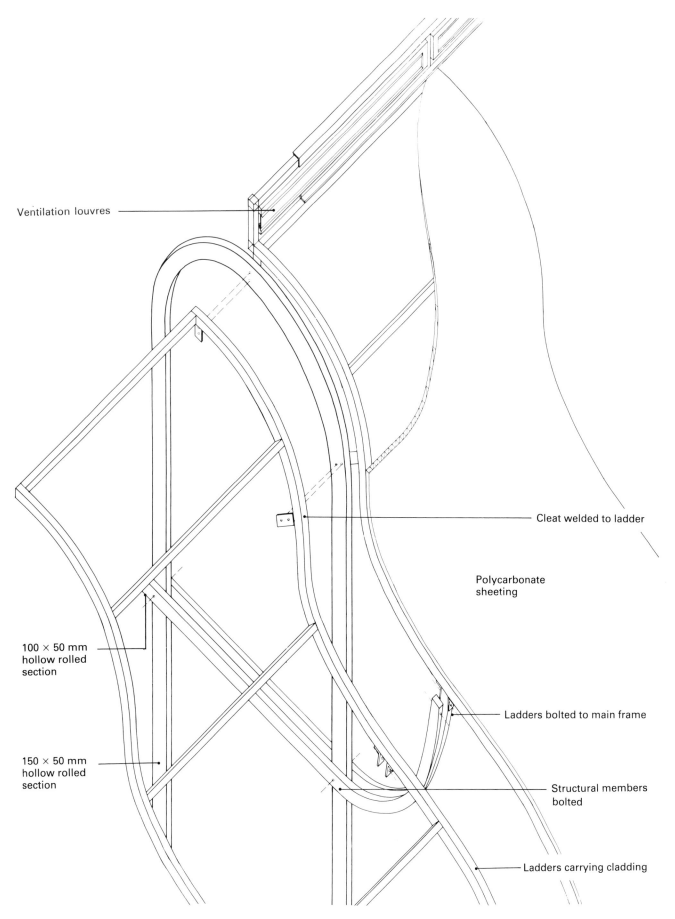

Ventilation louvres

Cleat welded to ladder

Polycarbonate
sheeting

100 × 50 mm
hollow rolled
section

Ladders bolted to main frame

150 × 50 mm
hollow rolled
section

Structural members
bolted

Ladders carrying cladding

Fig. 6.2 Ladder frames bolted to main frame (Courtesy of Tim Rogers)

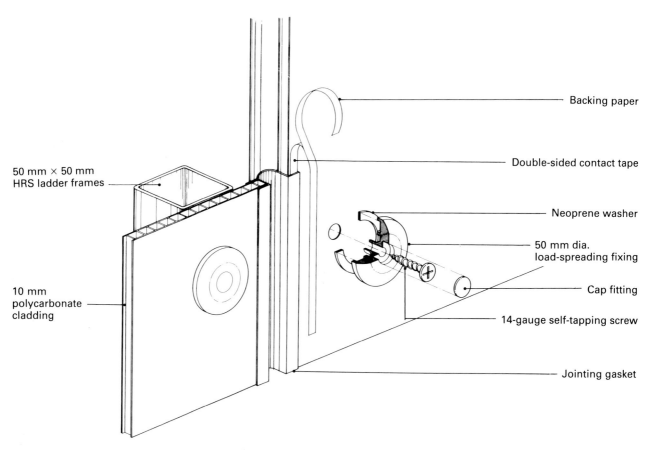

Fig. 6.3   Fixing of polycarbonate sheeting to ladder frames

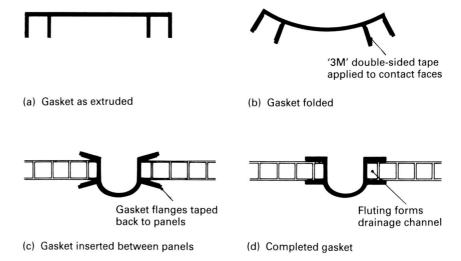

(a) Gasket as extruded

(b) Gasket folded

(c) Gasket inserted between panels

(d) Completed gasket

Fig. 6.4   Method of forming gasket seal

Further reading

1. Allinson, K & Ayres, P (1980)
    'Colonnades Garden Centre', *Architects' Journal*, 1 Oct. 1980, 658–62

2. Brookes, A J (1983)
    'Cladding and sealants', *Architects' Journal Supplement*, 29 June 1983, 24

3. Stevens, T (1980)
    'Inner city transplant', *Architects' Journal*, 25 June 1980, 1220–3

Case Study 7   Danish Embassy, Sloane Street, London

Fig. 7.1 Danish Embassy, Sloane Street, London (Courtesy of Brecht-Einzig Ltd)

General

Completed in September 1977, this unusual combination of aluminium panels, framed by *in situ* concrete, was subject to some changes in the design stages. The architects, Arne Jacobsen, Dissing and Weitling, originally intended to use bronze cladding, later changed to yellow-painted aluminium, and black granite walling later changed to patterned, *in situ* concrete.

Panels

The construction as built consists of 64 mm of mineral-fibre insulation board sandwiched between two layers of 16-gauge aluminium of 6 mm of asbestos sheet to improve flatness of the skin. The finish is a site-applied yellow acrylic paint.

It is interesting to note the inclusion of mild steel plates and channels at the window/panel junction, which may be a result of additional strength requirements for embassy buildings facing directly on to street facades.

Fig. 7.2 Close-up of panel (Courtesy of Brecht-Einzig Ltd)

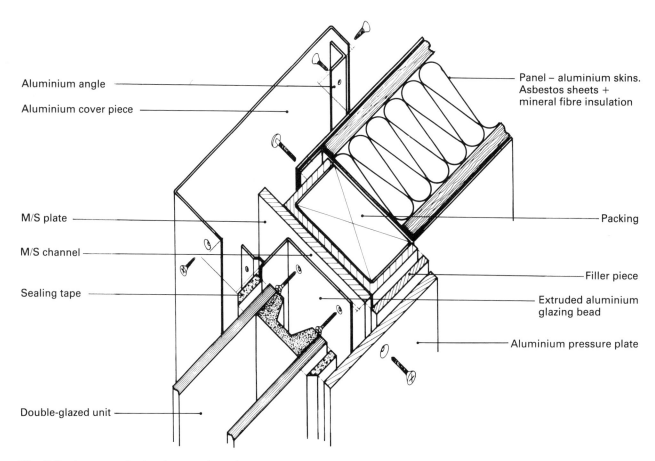

Aluminium angle

Aluminium cover piece

M/S plate

M/S channel

Sealing tape

Double-glazed unit

Panel – aluminium skins.
Asbestos sheets +
mineral fibre insulation

Packing

Filler piece

Extruded aluminium
glazing bead

Aluminium pressure plate

Fig. 7.3 Axonometric showing panel to window joint (Courtesy of Chris Stone)

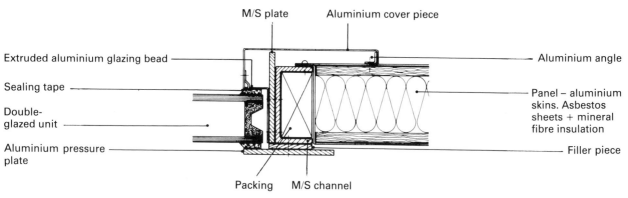

Fig. 7.4 Plan showing panel to window assembly (Courtesy of Tony Flannery)

Further reading

1. Brookes, A J (1983)
    Cladding of Buildings. Construction Press, London, 1983, p. 168

2. Brookes, A J & Ward, M (1981)
    'Art of construction — sheet metal systems — laminated panels',
    Architects' Journal, 8 July 1981, 84

3. Tye, Alan (1978)
    'Danish Embassy, London', *Architectural Review*, May 1978, 261–76

Case Study 8   The Festival Hall, Liverpool

Fig. 8.1 Internal view showing structure under construction

General

The Festival Hall in Liverpool served as a focus to the International Garden Festival, held during May to October 1984.

The building, designed by Arup Associates, was chosen as the winning entry in a national competition held in 1982. The client, Merseyside Development Corporation, required a multi-use exhibition space 8000 m², which would form a permanent feature of the south Liverpool waterfront, to be converted into a sports centre at a future date. One of the unusual aspects of the design is the vaulted steel roof, spanning 60 m, supporting a roof of transluscent double-skinned polycarbonate sheeting.

Domed ends

The two domed ends of the building are clad in profiled mill-finished aluminium sheets. Because of the form of the shell at these points, it was necessary to use a tapered profile, a product that is not readily available. British Aluminium's Special Products Division at their Falkirk Works undertook the manufacturing and developed the following press-brake process. Firstly, the sheet aluminium was hand sheared to size to ensure a high degree of dimensional accuracy. Then, each profile was individually pressed by aligning the sheet by hand against a stop. An A7 tapered form was used, this being a standard product. Finally, the profiled sheets were curved to the correct radius, using a thin roll bender. The dimensions, curvature and profile spacing had to be varied, depending upon which part of the building the sheets were for, and the use of hand-finishing techniques ensured that all sheets fitted very well with a low rejection rate. This was a vital consideration on this job, where speed of erection was essential. The press brake used by BACO in the manufacture of these sheets can handle work up to a maximum length of 5 m.

The profiled aluminium sheets were then fixed to 63.5-mm diameter purlins with 80-mm rockwool insulation, 0.165-mm vapour barrier and aluminium acoustic liner panels used as the inner lining.

Polycarbonate sheeting

The long sheets of 16-mm double-walled polycarbonate 1 m wide were mounted on to an extruded PVC base section, supported by 180 mm by 120 mm pre-painted mild steel channel mullions, spanning between 90 mm by 90 mm RHS purlins at 3-m centres. The polycarbonate sheet manufactured by 'Makrolon' should never be screwed or riveted in place and thus the design evolved an extruded PVC clamping bar with neoprene sealing strips. An extruded colour-coated aluminium cover trim clipped over the jointing assembly on its outside face, to hide the fixing clamps.

One difficulty experienced by the sub-contractor fixers was that, due to the extremely light weight (2.7 kg per m^2) and long lengths, the sheets were blown by the wind during lifting and had to be held by guy ropes from the ground and lifted into place. Even so, the roof skin was assembled very quickly indeed.

The ends of the polycarbonate sheeting are covered with an aluminium edge trim. It was necessary to clean out the spaces between the polycarbonate skins to prevent mould growth, particularly at the ridge of the roof.

Fig. 8.2 View of end bay showing construction using profiled aluminium sheeting

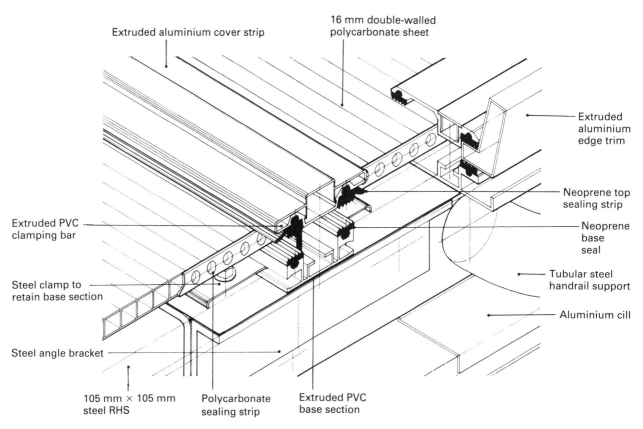

Extruded aluminium cover strip

16 mm double-walled polycarbonate sheet

Extruded aluminium edge trim

Neoprene top sealing strip

Neoprene base seal

Tubular steel handrail support

Aluminium cill

Extruded PVC clamping bar

Steel clamp to retain base section

Steel angle bracket

105 mm × 105 mm steel RHS

Polycarbonate sealing strip

Extruded PVC base section

Fig. 8.3 Cutaway section showing junction between polycarbonate sheets and eaves detail (Courtesy of Alf Plant)

Fig. 8.4 Detail of polycarbonate fixing

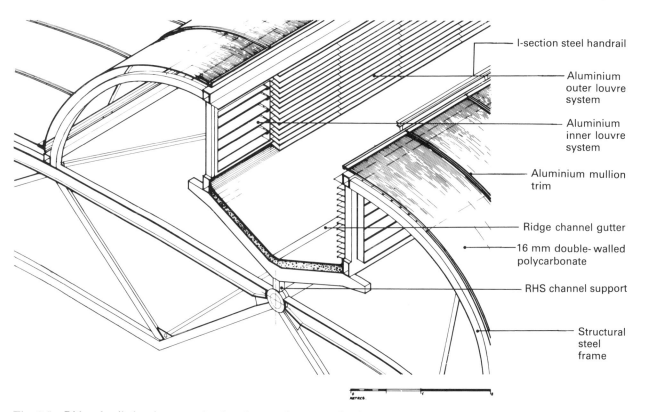

I-section steel handrail

Aluminium outer louvre system

Aluminium inner louvre system

Aluminium mullion trim

Ridge channel gutter

16 mm double-walled polycarbonate

RHS channel support

Structural steel frame

Fig. 8.5 Ridge detail showing curved polycarbonate sheets meeting louvre system

Fig. 8.6 Detail of structure under construction (Photo by Alf Plant)

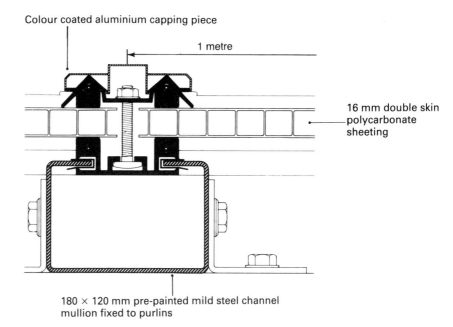

Colour coated aluminium capping piece

1 metre

16 mm double skin polycarbonate sheeting

180 × 120 mm pre-painted mild steel channel mullion fixed to purlins

Fig. 8.7 Section through polycarbonate to mullion junction (Courtesy of '*Building*')

Further reading

1. Anon
   'Arup dome', *Architectural Review*, June 1984, 29–31

2. Williams, A (1984)
   'Liverpool Festival Hall', *Building*, 27 April 1984, 43–9

3. Williams, S (1984)
   'Showplaces to play in', *Building Design Roofing Supplement*, 30 Mar. 1984

Case Study 9

Fleetguard Factory, Quimper, Brittany, France

Fig. 9.1 Corner view showing external structure (Photo by Ken Kirkwood)

General

The Fleetguard Factory, designed by Richard Rogers and Partners, is probably best known for its tall, red masts and web of suspension cables. This two-way spanning innovative structure (Engineers: Ove Arup and Partners) is braced by diagonal props at each end of the building so that each bay is independent of the one adjacent to it. The system of cladding, using PVf2 silver-coated profiled steel, mounted on rectangular hollow-section cladding posts, deserves more detailed inspection.

37

Cladding

The cladding detail, derived from that used at Greene King Brewery (see case study 10) used profiled sheet-steel cladding fixed to the rectangular cladding posts and joined using an extruded aluminium cover strip to hide the vertical joint. Although the vertical joint detail is similar to that of Greene King Brewery, the types of profiles used and their relative spans are quite different and reflect the particular architect's aesthetic intentions. At Greene King, the deep Plannja profile 50 spans 6 m between vertical supports. Here, the finer Plannja type 20B spans only 2 m between vertical supports.

The profiled sheet, supplied by Plannja Dobel Ltd and fixed by Chagnas Construction Metallique, was finished in silver PVf2 externally and used perforated steel sheet coated in white acrylic internally. Contained between the two profiled sheets is 50-mm 'Rockwool' insulation and a vapour barrier. A glazed strip round the top of the cladding allows light and a view of the sky on to the shop floor and, more importantly, lightens the building's feel. A similar concept of a glazed strip was originally anticipated for Foster's Renault factory (see case study 21) which also uses a suspension structure but had to be abandoned due to the high deflections at the edge beam. At Fleetguard, a sliding connection at the head of the cladding takes account of similar deflections.

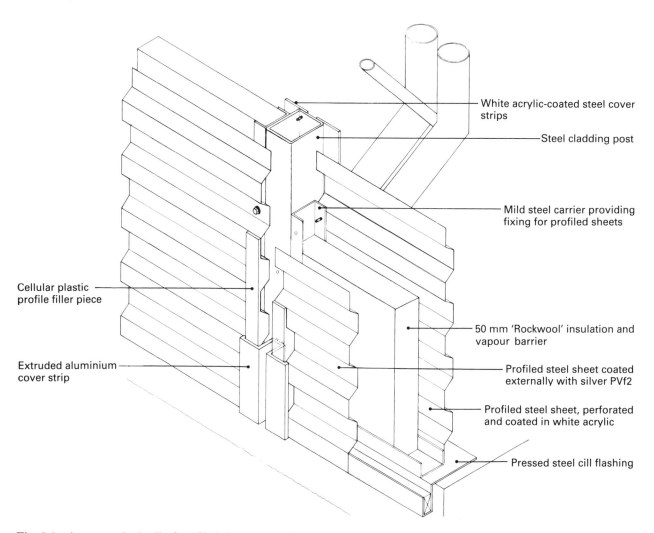

White acrylic-coated steel cover strips

Steel cladding post

Mild steel carrier providing fixing for profiled sheets

Cellular plastic profile filler piece

50 mm 'Rockwool' insulation and vapour barrier

Extruded aluminium cover strip

Profiled steel sheet coated externally with silver PVf2

Profiled steel sheet, perforated and coated in white acrylic

Pressed steel cill flashing

Fig. 9.2 Axonometric detail of profiled sheet to cladding post (Courtesy of Malcolm Jenkins)

Fig. 9.3   Overall view of horizontal profiled sheeting (Photo by Ken Kirkwood)

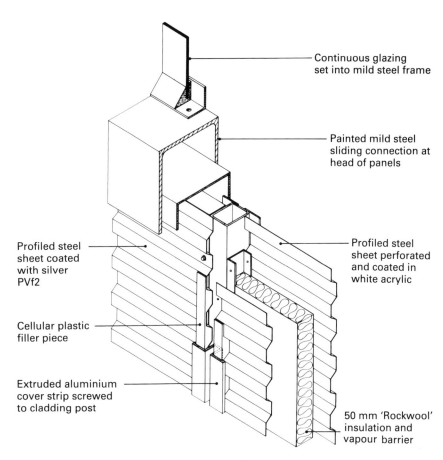

Continuous glazing
set into mild steel frame

Painted mild steel
sliding connection at
head of panels

Profiled steel
sheet perforated
and coated in
white acrylic

50 mm 'Rockwool'
insulation and
vapour barrier

Profiled steel
sheet coated
with silver
PVf2

Cellular plastic
filler piece

Extruded aluminium
cover strip screwed
to cladding post

Fig. 9.4   Head detail showing continuous channel

39

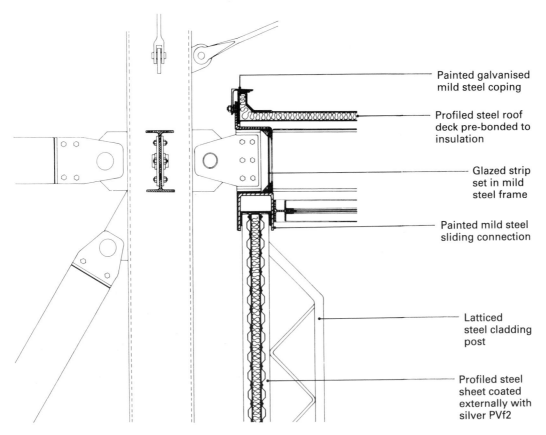

Painted galvanised mild steel coping

Profiled steel roof deck pre-bonded to insulation

Glazed strip set in mild steel frame

Painted mild steel sliding connection

Latticed steel cladding post

Profiled steel sheet coated externally with silver PVf2

Fig. 9.5 Section through eaves

Further reading

1. Ackermann, K (1984)
    'Industriebau' Deutsche Verlags-Anstalt, Stuttgart 1984, 200–5
2. Knobel, L (1982)
    'Factory, Quimper, Brittany, France', *Architectural Review*, Feb. 1982, 25–30

Case Study 10   Greene King Brewery, Draught Beer Plant, Bury St Edmunds, Suffolk

Fig. 10.1   General corner view showing aluminium glazed doors by Crawford Door Ltd, and matching profiled steel cladding by Plannja Dobel (Courtesy of Ken Kirkwood)

General

The draught beer plant for Greene King Brewery, designed by Michael Hopkins Architects, displays an elegance created by the skilful contrast between the open-glazed loading bays, with their cantilevered roof overhang and the silver PVf2 coated profiled steel sides. The building received an RIBA award, structural steel design award and *Financial Times* industrial architecture award during 1980.

Due to risk from flooding, the concrete floor slab was raised to be at tail-board height for lorries, which also allows a large building to perch lightly on its site. The steel frame, designed by Anthony Hunt Associates, consists of three rows of circular columns, supporting deep-trussed roof beams with a small cantilever on each side.

The cladding

The profiled silver PVf2 finished steel cladding (Plannja 50) runs horizontally inside and outside, supported by 200 mm by 100 mm rectangular hollow-section steel cladding posts, spanning between floor and edge beam. An extruded aluminium cover strip is screwed to the cladding post positioned at intervals, two to every structural bay. Lengths of horizontal profiled cladding are thus 6-m spanning between cladding posts and fixed at their end into a mild steel angle, welded to the cladding post and based in the centre of the span by an intermediate post.

Insulation consists of 60-mm thick paper-faced fibreglass, retained by small angle secured to RHS. Fixings, 500-mm centres approximately. The loading bay facade consists of fully-glazed sectional overhead doors and matching fixed panel areas by Crawford Door Ltd, in their 'Aluflex' system, manufactured from aluminium extrusions and insulated 342 system panels.

41

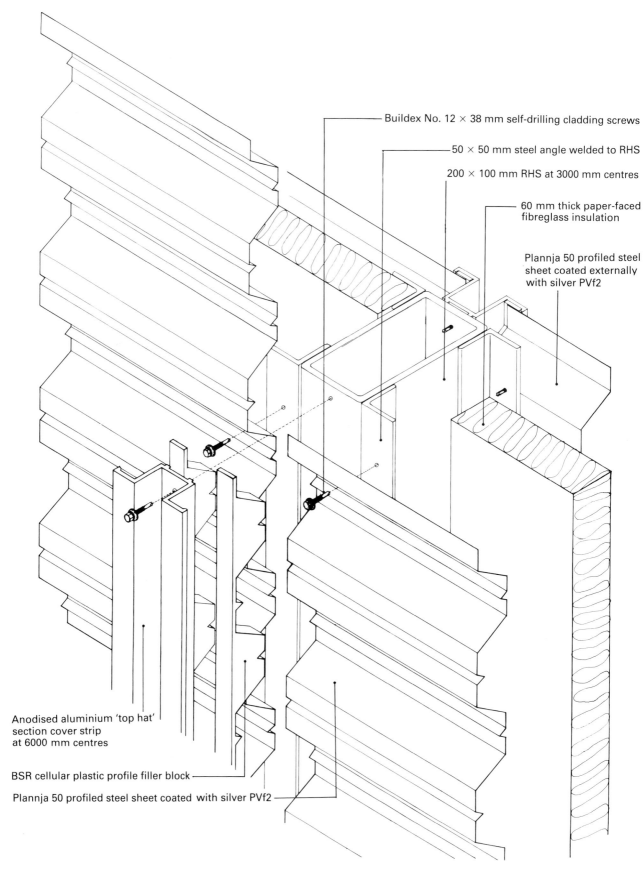

Buildex No. 12 × 38 mm self-drilling cladding screws

50 × 50 mm steel angle welded to RHS

200 × 100 mm RHS at 3000 mm centres

60 mm thick paper-faced fibreglass insulation

Plannja 50 profiled steel sheet coated externally with silver PVf2

Anodised aluminium 'top hat' section cover strip at 6000 mm centres

BSR cellular plastic profile filler block

Plannja 50 profiled steel sheet coated with silver PVf2

Fig. 10.2 Axonometric detail through profiled cladding showing 'top hat' cover strip jointing detail (Courtesy of Malcolm Jenkins)

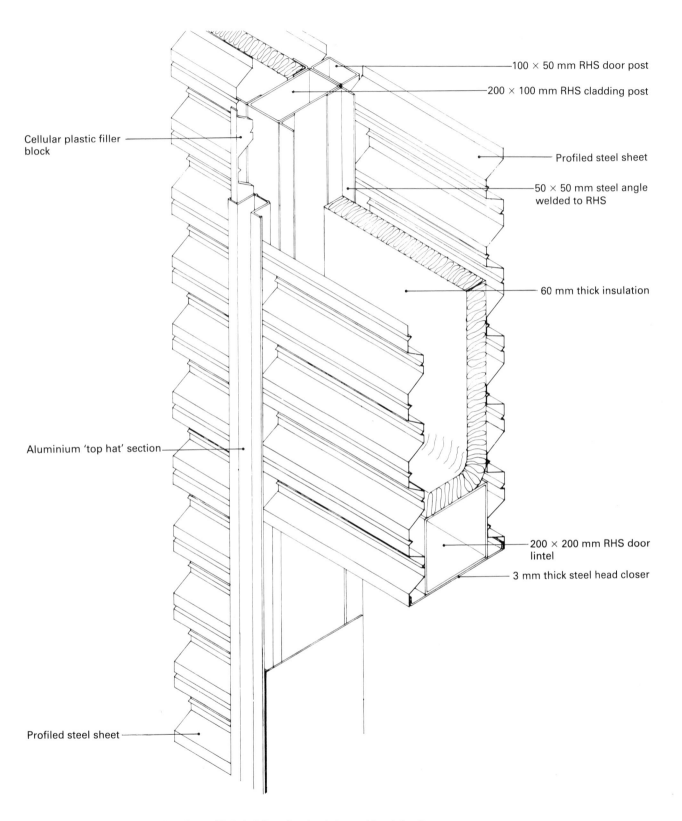

Cellular plastic filler block

100 × 50 mm RHS door post

200 × 100 mm RHS cladding post

Profiled steel sheet

50 × 50 mm steel angle welded to RHS

60 mm thick insulation

Aluminium 'top hat' section

200 × 200 mm RHS door lintel

3 mm thick steel head closer

Profiled steel sheet

Fig. 10.3 Unloading bay door in profiled cladding showing joint and head detail

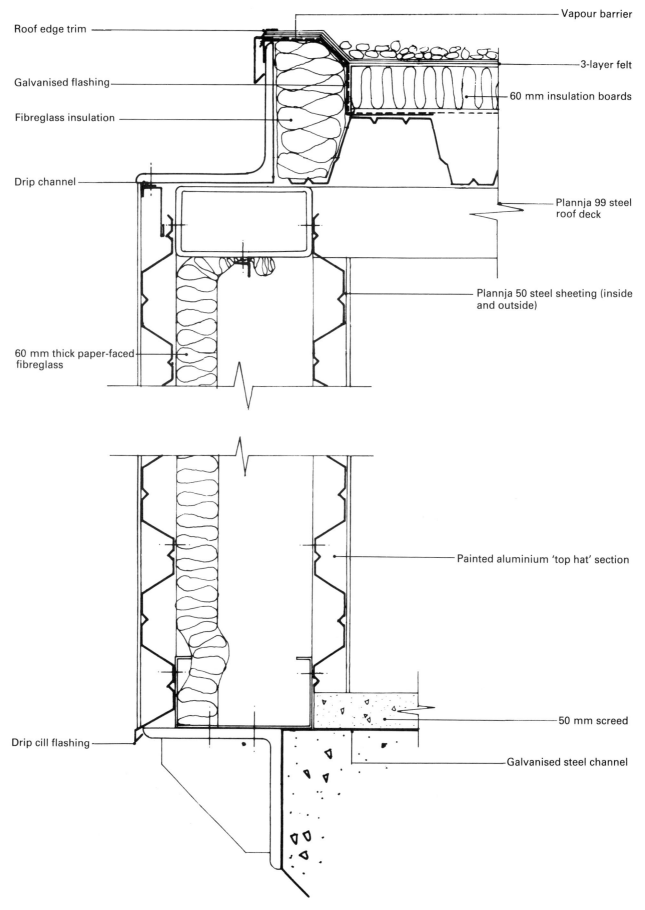

Vapour barrier

Roof edge trim

Galvanised flashing

Fibreglass insulation

3-layer felt

60 mm insulation boards

Drip channel

Plannja 99 steel roof deck

Plannja 50 steel sheeting (inside and outside)

60 mm thick paper-faced fibreglass

Painted aluminium 'top hat' section

50 mm screed

Drip cill flashing

Galvanised steel channel

Fig. 10.4 Section through profiled steel side walls

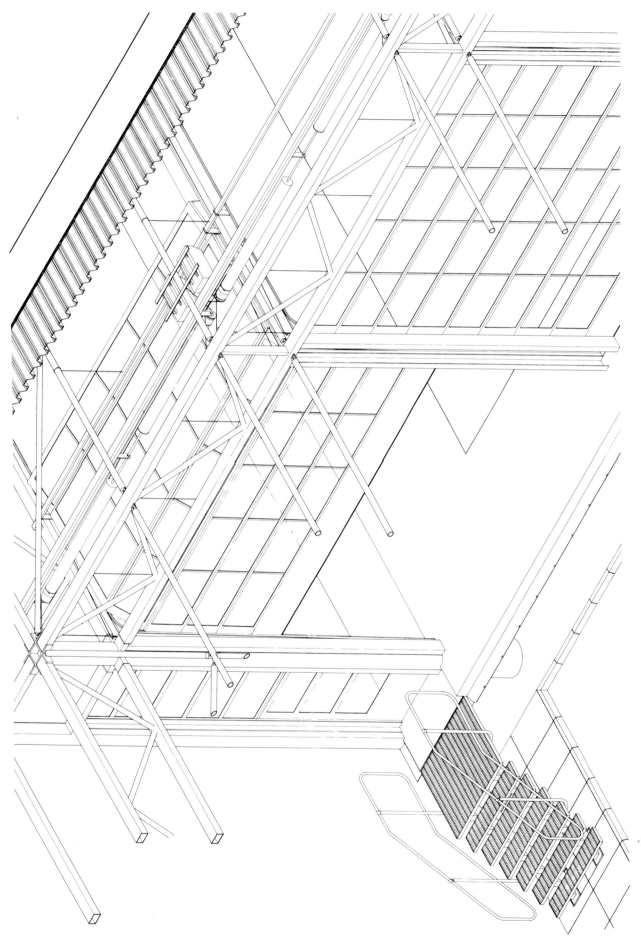

Fig. 10.5 Cutaway isometric of glazed doors (Courtesy of Michael Hopkins Architects)

Further reading

1. Anon (1980)
    'Greene King Westgate Brewery', *RIBA Journal*, Aug. 1980, 42

2. Anon (1980)
    'Interiors — the spotless brewery', *Design (London) 1980*, Dec., 56–8

3. Anon (1980)
    'Greene greener greenest', *Building*, 5 Dec. 1980, 14

4. Davies, C (1984)
    'Hopkin's rules', *Architectural Review*, May 1984, 54–7

5. Winter, J (1981)
    'Racking in Suffolk', *Architectural Review*, Mar. 1981, 146–50

6. Also, articles contained in:
    Baumeister, Vol. 80, No. 4, Apr. 1983, 330–1; *Techniques and Architecture*, No. 342, June 1982, 116–17

Case Study 11 Herman Miller Factory, Bath

Fig. 11.1 Overall view of building facing river (Courtesy of Joe Reid and John Peck)

General

Designed for the Herman Miller Furniture Company by the Farrell Grimshaw Partnership and occupied in 1977, the Herman Miller Factory is situated on the River Avon at Bath within an industrial area. A pedestrian bridge links it to an earlier Yorke, Rosenberg and Mardall office block across the river.

The GRP panels are cream coloured to harmonise with the Bath stone, the predominant material in the city. Tinted glass is either in fixed panels or louvre windows. All produce a building of great charm with the best side by the river landscaped with trees and furniture for sitting out. The essential feature of this design is the use of lightweight interchangeable panels and glazing, allowing total flexibility of the external cladding with a constant horizontal and vertical joint detail capable of accepting any sheet material up to 6 mm thick. Insulated double-skin glass-fibre panels have the same dimensions as glazed panels, so all are interchangeable.

GRP panels

The 1250 mm by 3000 mm GRP panels form the main cladding element. Manufactured by Artech Plastics (no longer in business), they consist of two separate insulated sandwiches with an air gap between. Each sandwich was constructed from two skins of GRP bonded to an insulating core of sprayed-on polyurethane foam. The edge of the panel was formed by bringing the two laminates together (see Fig. 11.2).

A simple pressure-glazing technique using a neoprene gasket mounted on a 'top hat' aluminium beading member then fixes the panels back on to an aluminium carrier system which is, in turn, supported by the main box-section steel frame. The detail does not include a 'zipper' gasket, as is often supposed. The design of the gasket was specially developed for this project by Modern Art Glass Company Limited in conjunction with Leyland and Birmingham Rubber Company and Aluminium Systems, Dublin.

Cladding frame

The cladding frame consists of 125 mm by 100 mm rectangular hollow-section steel tubes spanning the full 6-m height between the floor slab to the steel I-section edge beam. Spacing rails then span 1.12 m between the verticals at the top, bottom and mid-points, thus providing a grid of 1250 mm by 3000 mm on to which can be fitted GRP panels, glazed panels, louvre panels or glazed doors.

Carrier system and gasket

The detail shows an aluminium carrier system, by Modern Art Glass, fixed back to the external face of the cladding frame with the top hat aluminium section, holding the neoprene gasket, screwed into the carrier. Thus a mechanical joint is formed on all sides of the panel. The top hat section is mitred at the corners and the preformed neoprene gaskets were produced by the Leyland and Birmingham Rubber Company Limited, with injection-moulded corners to form a continuous window frame. Due to difficulties at that time in forming the aluminium carrier to a curve, it was not possible to provide a gasket joint between the curved GRP parapet panels, and the joint changes here to a narrower mastic sealant. A pressed-metal flashing was used at ground level.

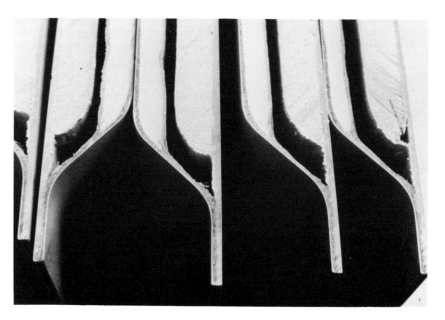

Fig. 11.2   Sectioned view of GRP panels showing double-foamed cores

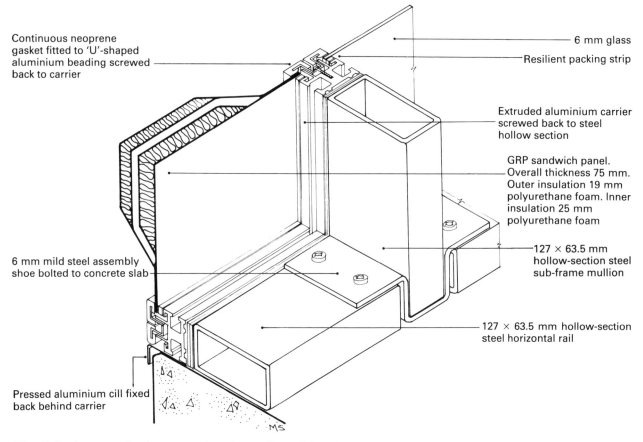

Continuous neoprene gasket fitted to 'U'-shaped aluminium beading screwed back to carrier

6 mm glass

Resilient packing strip

Extruded aluminium carrier screwed back to steel hollow section

GRP sandwich panel. Overall thickness 75 mm. Outer insulation 19 mm polyurethane foam. Inner insulation 25 mm polyurethane foam

6 mm mild steel assembly shoe bolted to concrete slab

127 × 63.5 mm hollow-section steel sub-frame mullion

127 × 63.5 mm hollow-section steel horizontal rail

Pressed aluminium cill fixed back behind carrier

Fig. 11.3 Axonometric of cross-over junction at cill condition (Courtesy of M. Saunders)

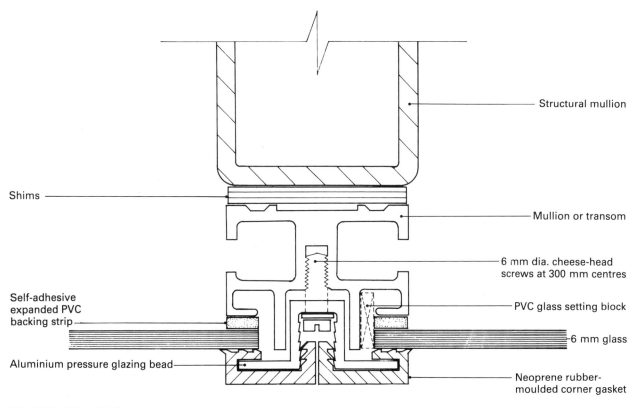

Shims

Structural mullion

Mullion or transom

6 mm dia. cheese-head screws at 300 mm centres

Self-adhesive expanded PVC backing strip

PVC glass setting block

6 mm glass

Aluminium pressure glazing bead

Neoprene rubber-moulded corner gasket

Fig. 11.4 Plan of joint

49

Further reading

1. Anon (1977)
   'Miller on Avon', *Domus*, No. 576, 24 Nov. 1977, 20–2

2. Anon (1977)
   'Action factory', *RIBA Journal*, No. 84, Sept. 1977, 377–83

3. Anon (1978)
   'Building Study Herman Miller Factory', *Architects' Journal*, Vol. 167, No. 9, 1 Mar. 1978, 395–407

4. Brookes, A J (1980)
   'Claddings — product selection and specification', *Architects' Journal*, Vol. 172, No. 45, 5 Nov. 1980, 906–7

5. Brookes, A J & Ward, M (1981)
   'Art of construction, GRP claddings — Part 2 Panel design', *Architects' Journal*, 17 June 1981, 1173–4

6. Drury, J (1981)
   Factories, Planning Design and Modernisation. Architectural Press, London, 1981, p. 231

Case Study 12 Herman Miller Warehouse, Chippenham, near Bath

Fig. 12.1 Overall view of warehouse

General

The Herman Miller warehouse is located on the outskirts of Chippenham, close to the Bath Road and the main London to Bristol railway line. The building, completed in 1983, represents the first of three eventual phases. Designed by Nicholas Grimshaw Partnership (job architect Neven Sidor) and engineered by Peter Brett Associates, the building is an example of the clip-together modular interchangeable component design aesthetic.

The aluminium panels, manufactured by Kinain Workshops and fixed by R. M. Douglas, are finished in 'Syntha Pulvin' polyester powder applied by Acorn Anodising Company Limited, Hayes, Middlesex.

Cladding

Solid panels, fixed windows, fire doors and personnel doors may be unbolted and moved to any location on a 2.4 m by 1.2 m grid, while the four apertures in each window frame offer additional flexibility for ventilation louvres and service outlet panels.

Figure 12.1 shows doubled pairs of 'Unistrut' channels (type P1001), spanning vertically between cladding rails. This provides a secondary support system, which includes provision for bolted fixings at any point up to the height of each of the channels. The panels are face fixed through to the 'Unistrut' channel, using stainless steel bolts held within the channel by a sprung nut, with continuous black extruded sections of neoprene between

51

the panel and its channel support forming the vertical joint. The horizontal joint is formed by each higher panel overlapping the lower one and stiffened by a special 'T' bar, which also acts as a ladder rail.

The 2.4 m by 1.2 m aluminium panels were stamped in one operation using an interlocking die section to form each of the moulded profiles. Twelve interlocking sections were thus used to produce the die for each panel. Panels are insulated using 50-mm thick 'Rockwool' roof decking slab, cut to fit inside a perforated steel internal cladding panel liner tray (finished in white).

Most panels have an external finish in light blue (5102) 'Syntha Pulvin' polyester powder coating. External 'pod' structures are finished in dark blue (5010) and the 'T' bar extrusions are finished in cobalt blue (5003).

Neoprene jointing

The neoprene jointing extrusions were not brought to the site predrilled, as reported by Lyall[2]. Originally, it was intended that the drilling should take place on site from a single template on the ground. In the event, it proved easier, due to some stretching of the neoprene, to use a dummy panel as a template in position on the 'Unistrut' supports.

The designer intending to use this principle of jointing should also be aware of the need to anticipate the inaccuracy during construction in the alignment of the vertical 'Unistruts' and the neoprene gasket should be designed with flanges that take this into consideration, thus allowing the panels to be bolted fully home.

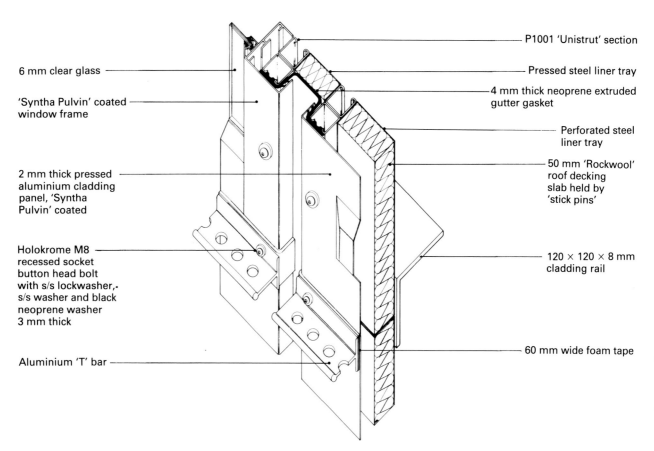

6 mm clear glass

'Syntha Pulvin' coated window frame

2 mm thick pressed aluminium cladding panel, 'Syntha Pulvin' coated

Holokrome M8 recessed socket button head bolt with s/s lockwasher, s/s washer and black neoprene washer 3 mm thick

Aluminium 'T' bar

P1001 'Unistrut' section

Pressed steel liner tray

4 mm thick neoprene extruded gutter gasket

Perforated steel liner tray

50 mm 'Rockwool' roof decking slab held by 'stick pins'

120 × 120 × 8 mm cladding rail

60 mm wide foam tape

Fig. 12.2 Axonometric detail of panel to panel connection (Courtesy of S. Boobyer)

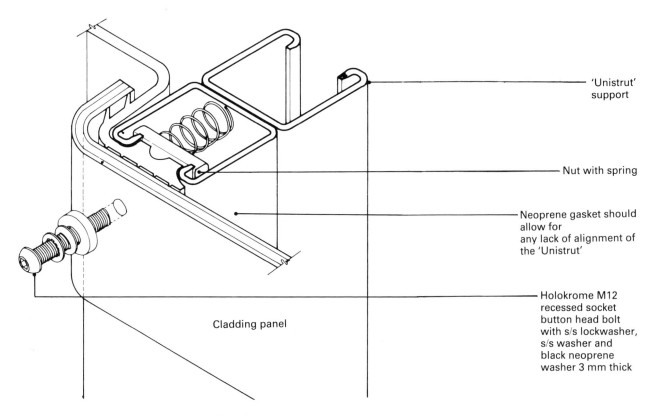

'Unistrut' support

Nut with spring

Neoprene gasket should allow for any lack of alignment of the 'Unistrut'

Holokrome M12 recessed socket button head bolt with s/s lockwasher, s/s washer and black neoprene washer 3 mm thick

Cladding panel

Fig. 12.3   View of panel fixing to 'Unistrut' support

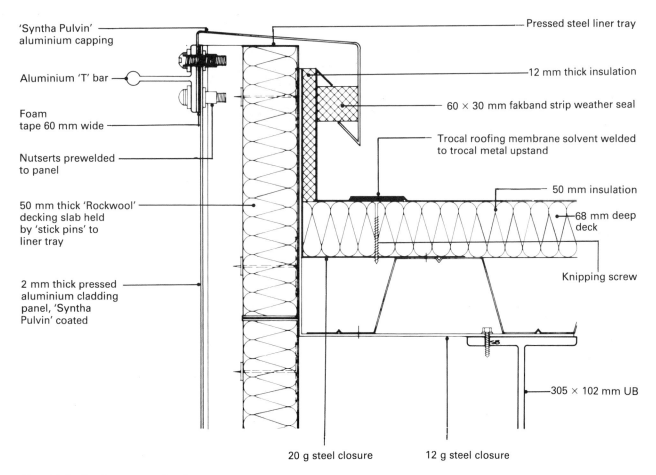

'Syntha Pulvin' aluminium capping

Aluminium 'T' bar

Foam tape 60 mm wide

Nutserts prewelded to panel

50 mm thick 'Rockwool' decking slab held by 'stick pins' to liner tray

2 mm thick pressed aluminium cladding panel, 'Syntha Pulvin' coated

Pressed steel liner tray

12 mm thick insulation

60 × 30 mm fakband strip weather seal

Trocal roofing membrane solvent welded to trocal metal upstand

50 mm insulation

68 mm deep deck

Knipping screw

305 × 102 mm UB

20 g steel closure   12 g steel closure

Fig. 12.4   Section at eaves level

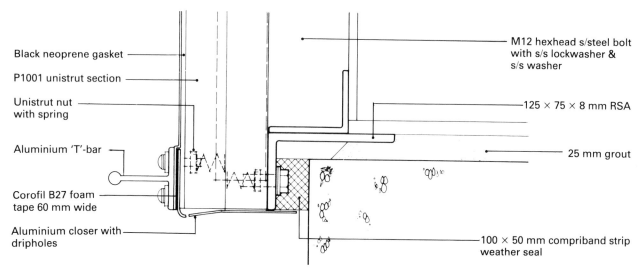

Black neoprene gasket

P1001 unistrut section

Unistrut nut
with spring

Aluminium 'T'-bar

Corofil B27 foam
tape 60 mm wide

Aluminium closer with
dripholes

M12 hexhead s/steel bolt
with s/s lockwasher &
s/s washer

125 × 75 × 8 mm RSA

25 mm grout

100 × 50 mm compriband strip
weather seal

Fig. 12.5   Section at floor level

Fig. 12.6   View of aluminium panels showing profiling of surface

Further reading

1.   Atkinson, G (1984)
     'Mastering the movement', *Building*, 17 Feb. 1984

2.   Lyall, Sutherland (1983)
     'Engineered for elegance', *Building*, 30 Sept. 1983, 35–7

3. Murray, Peter (1983)
    'Herman Miller at Chippenham', *RIBA Journal*, Sept. 1983, 59–66
4. Stevens, Ted (1983)
    'Grimshaw scores a double top', *Building Design*, 22 Apr. 1983, 16–19

Case Study 13 Hochhaus Dresdner Bank AG, Frankfurt/Main, Germany

Fig. 13.1 Overall view of building (Courtesy of Josef Gartner & Co)

General

The Hochhaus Dresdner Bank in Frankfurt, designed by Becker and Becker and Partner and completed in 1979, represents an unusually high quality, and therefore comparatively high cost, of detailing and use of materials. This tall tower block, standing in the centre of Frankfurt, is clad completely in natural silver anodised-aluminium panels, manufactured by Josef Gartner. The total height of the building is 166 m and the total area is 36 000 mm².

Cladding

The storey-height aluminium panels, 4200 mm high by 1800 mm wide, consist of 2.5-mm aluminium rolled sheet outer skin, which has been deep drawn in the form of a tray and screwed to an aluminium carrier system. At a junction between two panels, the carrier is in four sections, forming the outer and inner parts of the assembly. The outer section, which is separated by means of thermal breaks from the inner section, supports the aluminium outer skin. The inner section supports the insulation panel and inner lining. The complete assembly is bolted back to the main framing, which in turn is supported by the *in situ* slab.

The panels include double-glazed window units (toughened glass type Calorex IRA 0). Aluminium window screens, column claddings and revolving doors are at ground-floor level. A link bridge connects the new tower to the existing building and is glazed with bronze anodised-aluminium cladding.

Jointing

In order to protect them from ultra-violet light, the neoprene gasket seals are hidden within the assembly. The joint expression on the outer face is a wide gap, approximately the width of a standard photographic film box. The complexity of the aluminium section allows both inner and outer seals. The 100-mm wide groove within the joint also acts as a drainage channel before the 'primary seal'.

This joint, albeit a complex form, demonstrates many of the principles related to interchangeable curtain wall/panel systems used today, namely that the panels are supported by the aluminium carrier system, which is, in turn, fixed to the main structural framing. In this respect, it does not differ from the carrier systems used at the Herman Miller Factory at Bath (see case study 11) or even the proprietary system used at Chester-le-Street (see case study 5) although, obviously, these are less complex and, therefore, less costly versions of this theme.

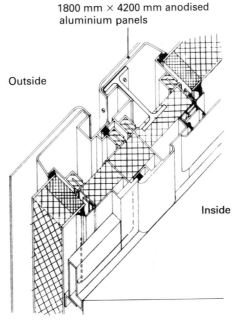

1800 mm × 4200 mm anodised aluminium panels

Outside

Inside

Fig. 13.2 Axonometric view of panels fixed back to structure (Courtesy of Peter Franklin)

Fig. 13.3 View looking up facade (Courtesy of Josef Gartner & Co)

Fig. 13.4 Panels over main entrance

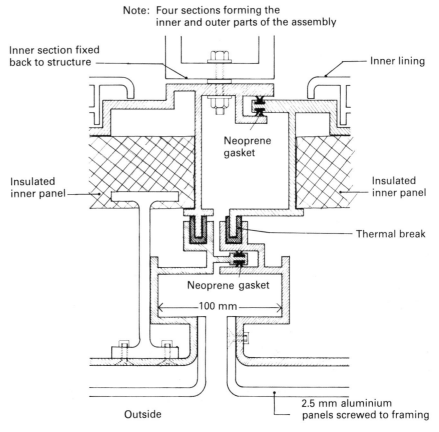

Fig. 13.5 Plan of joint

Fig. 13.6 Showing stiffening ribs welded to curved corner panels

Further reading

1. Brookes, A J & Ward, M (1981)
   'The art of construction — metal claddings — case studies', *Architects' Journal*, 15 July 1981, 121

2. Josef Gartner Calendar (1980)
   Jan. 1980

Case Study 14 IBM Midlands Marketing Centre, Warwick

Fig. 14.1 Overall view of building

General

The IBM Midlands Marketing Centre at Birmingham Road, Warwick, designed by Yorke, Rosenburg and Mardall, Architects and Planners, was completed in 1979. The Centre consists of two adjacent and connected buildings, a single-storey computer services centre and a two-storey marketing centre. Although the single-storey building has a steel frame (180 mm by 180 mm hollow-section steel column painted) and the two-storey building has a reinforced concrete frame (350 mm by 350 mm reinforced concrete column with 12-mm plaster finish), the elevational treatments are similar.

Cladding

A modular panel system for cladding was selected to satisfy the client's brief requirement for a flexible, interchangeable skin. The elevations incorporate white vitreous-enamel steel panels, manufactured by Escol Panels, Wellingborough, with black silicone joints and bronze double-glazed units in black-stoved acrylic aluminium frames. Louvres are painted pressed metal.

The panels, 1800 mm by 1200 mm, are in 1.6-mm thick vitreous-enamel steel with 12-mm asbestos-board backing, bonded to 30-mm mineral-fibre insulation faced with a foil-backed vapour barrier.

Sealant joint

Silicone jointing between the panels is set back 10 mm. However, according to Winter[1], dirt washed out of this recess adds to that on the panel face.

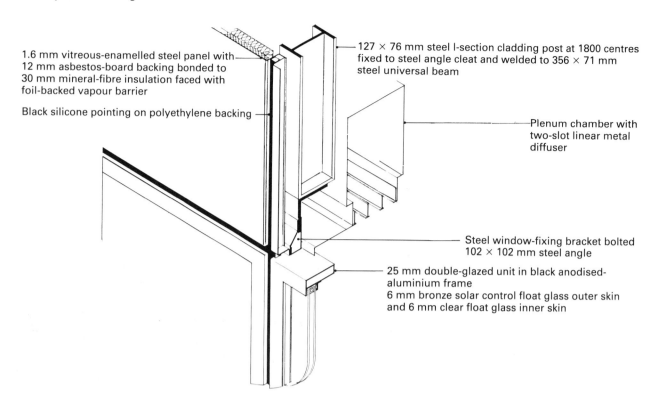

1.6 mm vitreous-enamelled steel panel with 12 mm asbestos-board backing bonded to 30 mm mineral-fibre insulation faced with foil-backed vapour barrier

Black silicone pointing on polyethylene backing

127 × 76 mm steel I-section cladding post at 1800 centres fixed to steel angle cleat and welded to 356 × 71 mm steel universal beam

Plenum chamber with two-slot linear metal diffuser

Steel window-fixing bracket bolted 102 × 102 mm steel angle

25 mm double-glazed unit in black anodised-aluminium frame
6 mm bronze solar control float glass outer skin and 6 mm clear float glass inner skin

Fig. 14.2 Axonometric view at cross-over between panels and windows, horizontal and vertical joints (Courtesy of John Hampton)

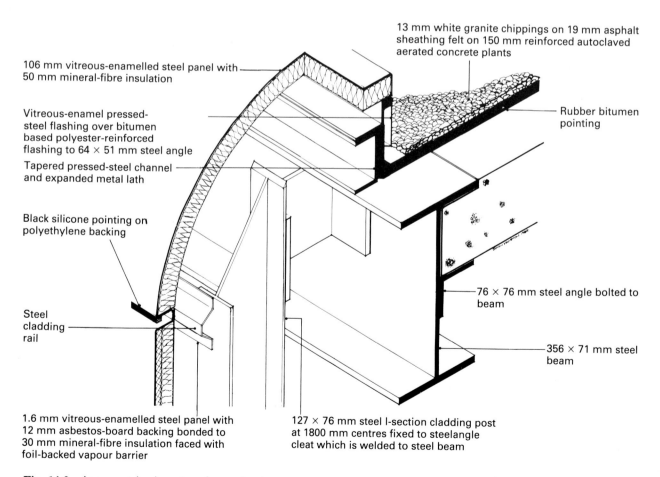

106 mm vitreous-enamelled steel panel with 50 mm mineral-fibre insulation

Vitreous-enamel pressed-steel flashing over bitumen based polyester-reinforced flashing to 64 × 51 mm steel angle

Tapered pressed-steel channel and expanded metal lath

Black silicone pointing on polyethylene backing

Steel cladding rail

13 mm white granite chippings on 19 mm asphalt sheathing felt on 150 mm reinforced autoclaved aerated concrete plants

Rubber bitumen pointing

76 × 76 mm steel angle bolted to beam

356 × 71 mm steel beam

1.6 mm vitreous-enamelled steel panel with 12 mm asbestos-board backing bonded to 30 mm mineral-fibre insulation faced with foil-backed vapour barrier

127 × 76 mm steel I-section cladding post at 1800 mm centres fixed to steelangle cleat which is welded to steel beam

Fig. 14.3 Axonometric view at roof eaves level

Fig. 14.4 Detail of corner panel

Further reading

1. Winter, John (1981)
   'Building study — IBM Midlands Marketing Centre, Warwick — appraisal', *Architects' Journal*, 18 Nov. 1981, 985–91

Case Study 15 IBM Sports Hall, Hursley Park, Winchester

Fig. 15.1 General view of Sports Centre (Courtesy of Crawford Door Ltd)

General

The brief for the new (1982) Sports Hall, located in the grounds of the IBM (UK) Ltd Laboratories at Hursley Park, outside Winchester, was to provide a multi-purpose Sports Hall, principally for playing badminton but also to be used for occasional social functions.

The architects, Nicholas Grimshaw and Partners, and structural engineers, F. J. Samuely and Partners, devised a striking design using five black space-frame portals, which support the walls and roof of the building and are expressed externally. The structure, which is designed for later expansion into nine bays, spans 18 m horizontally and 5.25 m vertically.

The roof, consisting of a lightweight Plannja 100-mm deep steel decking laid over purlins and supporting 50-mm insulation board, is suspended at the node points of the trusses with specially-designed turn-buckle connectors (see Fig. 15.2). These appear rather complicated compared with the nodus pin-joint connectors developed for the Patera system (see case study 20). The roof covering consists of a single-skin PVC sheet waterproof membrane with PVC collar sealing the points where the node points pierce the roof structure to connect with the roof purlins.

Cladding

The cladding is made up from Crawford insulated steel industrial 42-mm thick door panels, 5250 mm long and 500 mm high. These were bolted at their corners to cleats welded to the main frame and to the gable mullions. No cladding rail and no further secondary framing was required, other than cross-bracing between the trussed portal frames.

15-mm vertical joints between the panels were formed using a silicone 'firtree' gasket and the joint caulked from the inside using a silicone mastic seal.

The eaves and corner panels are formed from curved, double-skinned translucent blue GRP panels, similar to those used by the same architect at Winwick Quay 7, Warrington (see case study 30). These prefabricated panels, 1000 mm long by 42 mm thick, not only conveniently solve the corner detail but also provide natural daylight without glare. In the evening, the thin steel portals are silhouetted against the sky and the light shines through the blue translucent eaves and corner panels.

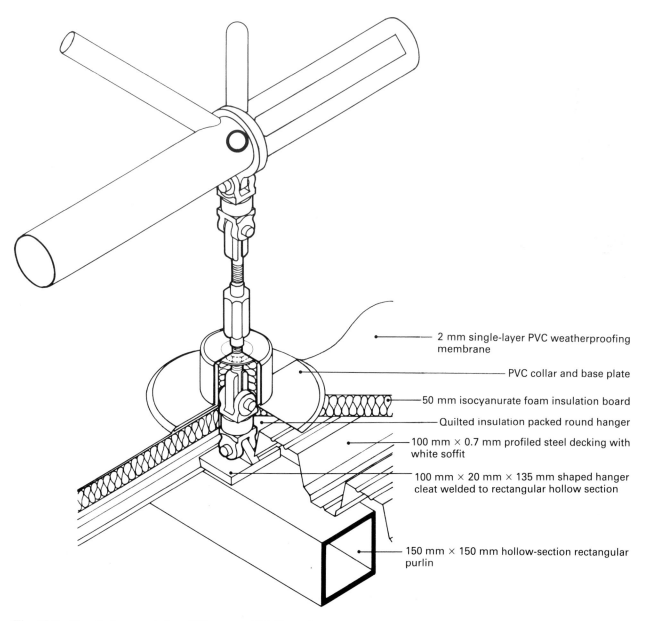

2 mm single-layer PVC weatherproofing membrane

PVC collar and base plate

50 mm isocyanurate foam insulation board

Quilted insulation packed round hanger

100 mm × 0.7 mm profiled steel decking with white soffit

100 mm × 20 mm × 135 mm shaped hanger cleat welded to rectangular hollow section

150 mm × 150 mm hollow-section rectangular purlin

Fig. 15.2   Detail of suspended roof (Courtesy of T. Turner)

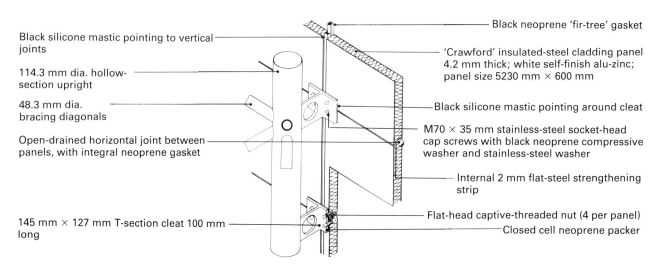

Black silicone mastic pointing to vertical joints

114.3 mm dia. hollow-section upright

48.3 mm dia. bracing diagonals

Open-drained horizontal joint between panels, with integral neoprene gasket

145 mm × 127 mm T-section cleat 100 mm long

Black neoprene 'fir-tree' gasket

'Crawford' insulated-steel cladding panel 4.2 mm thick; white self-finish alu-zinc; panel size 5230 mm × 600 mm

Black silicone mastic pointing around cleat

M70 × 35 mm stainless-steel socket-head cap screws with black neoprene compressive washer and stainless-steel washer

Internal 2 mm flat-steel strengthening strip

Flat-head captive-threaded nut (4 per panel)

Closed cell neoprene packer

Fig. 15.3 Detail of wall/frame junction

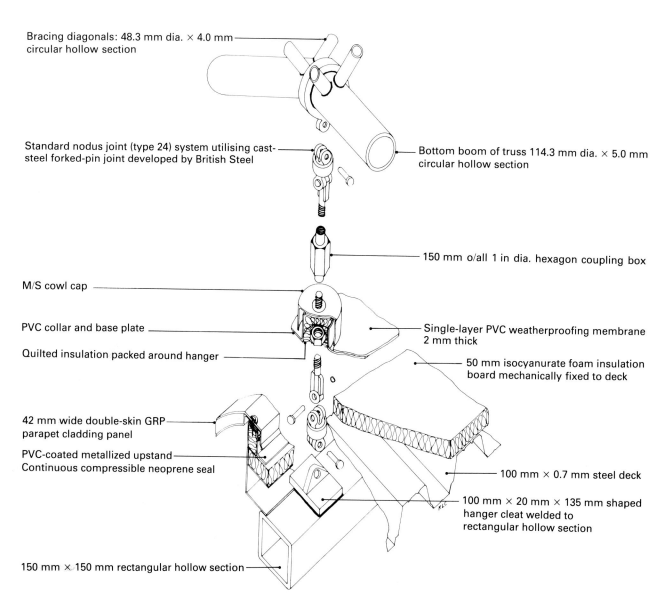

Bracing diagonals: 48.3 mm dia. × 4.0 mm circular hollow section

Standard nodus joint (type 24) system utilising cast-steel forked-pin joint developed by British Steel

M/S cowl cap

PVC collar and base plate

Quilted insulation packed around hanger

42 mm wide double-skin GRP parapet cladding panel

PVC-coated metallized upstand
Continuous compressible neoprene seal

150 mm × 150 mm rectangular hollow section

Bottom boom of truss 114.3 mm dia. × 5.0 mm circular hollow section

150 mm o/all 1 in dia. hexagon coupling box

Single-layer PVC weatherproofing membrane 2 mm thick

50 mm isocyanurate foam insulation board mechanically fixed to deck

100 mm × 0.7 mm steel deck

100 mm × 20 mm × 135 mm shaped hanger cleat welded to rectangular hollow section

Fig. 15.4 Exploded view of suspended roof (Courtesy of Karen Campbell)

66

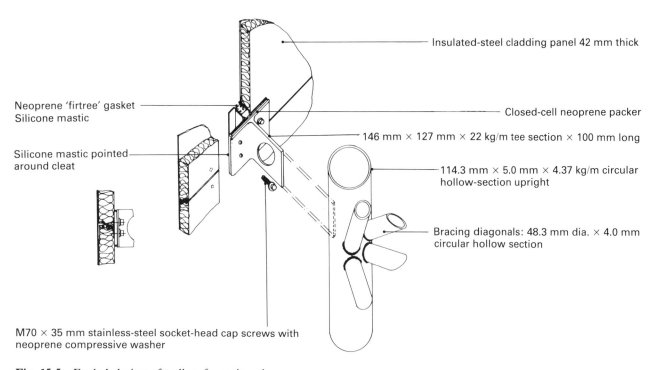

Insulated-steel cladding panel 42 mm thick

Neoprene 'firtree' gasket
Silicone mastic

Closed-cell neoprene packer

146 mm × 127 mm × 22 kg/m tee section × 100 mm long

Silicone mastic pointed
around cleat

114.3 mm × 5.0 mm × 4.37 kg/m circular
hollow-section upright

Bracing diagonals: 48.3 mm dia. × 4.0 mm
circular hollow section

M70 × 35 mm stainless-steel socket-head cap screws with
neoprene compressive washer

Fig. 15.5 Exploded view of wall to frame junction

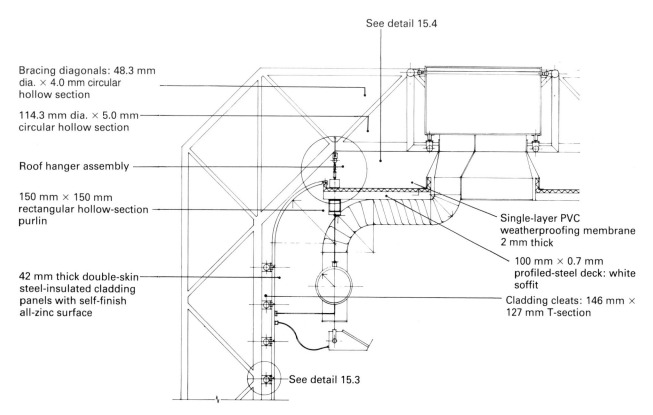

See detail 15.4

Bracing diagonals: 48.3 mm
dia. × 4.0 mm circular
hollow section

114.3 mm dia. × 5.0 mm
circular hollow section

Roof hanger assembly

150 mm × 150 mm
rectangular hollow-section
purlin

42 mm thick double-skin
steel-insulated cladding
panels with self-finish
all-zinc surface

Single-layer PVC
weatherproofing membrane
2 mm thick

100 mm × 0.7 mm
profiled-steel deck: white
soffit

Cladding cleats: 146 mm ×
127 mm T-section

See detail 15.3

Fig. 15.6 Section to external wall (Courtesy of Steve Meyer)

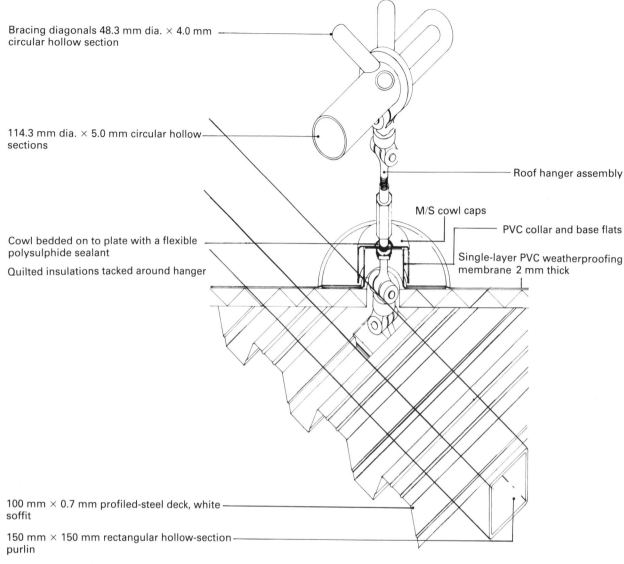

Bracing diagonals 48.3 mm dia. × 4.0 mm circular hollow section

114.3 mm dia. × 5.0 mm circular hollow sections

Roof hanger assembly

M/S cowl caps

PVC collar and base flats

Cowl bedded on to plate with a flexible polysulphide sealant

Single-layer PVC weatherproofing membrane 2 mm thick

Quilted insulations tacked around hanger

100 mm × 0.7 mm profiled-steel deck, white soffit

150 mm × 150 mm rectangular hollow-section purlin

Fig. 15.7 Detail of suspension system

Further reading

1. Papadakis, A C (1982)
   British Architecture. Architectural Design and A D Editions, 1982, pp. 74–6

2. Winter, J (1982)
   'Sports Centre, Hursley, Hants', *Architectural Review*, Mar. 1982, 34–41

Case Study 16　INMOS Microchip Factory, Newport, Gwent

Fig. 16.1　Overall view of building showing service pods

General

Originally designed for a site in Bristol, the INMOS microchip factory at Newport in Gwent, designed by Richard Rogers and Partners, represented 'fast track' design and build. The programme allowed just seven months from Rogers' appointment to setting up on site and fifteen months for completion of the production areas. The building was officially opened on 1 February 1982. The building design was conceived as a single-storey steel structure with a central linear circulation and service spine separating two column-free zones of production space. The tubular steel tension structure spanning 39 m is supported by tension rods from sets of spine towers. The steel trusses fabricated in Stratford-on-Avon by Tubeworkers Ltd were delivered to site in two halves and assembled and erected to form their full span. The roof is fabricated from 6-m span steel decking, with thermal insulation and a five-layer roof membrane.

In order to minimise deflection at the roof edge, the ends of the primary lattice trusses are stabilised by a combined tension and compression bipod.

Cladding

Within a design team of Rogers, Marco Goldschmeid and John Young, Pierre Botschi was responsible for wall cladding and roof decking.

The external walls are based on a standardised mullion and infill system by Jonwindows Ltd of Cardiff, which will accept any type of infill single glazing, double glazing translucent or opaque panels.

The composite insulated sandwich panels for the production area consist of two sheets of wallboard 'D' PVf2 finish, with 38-mm polyurethane core. Total thickness 46 mm. Double glazing on the office areas consists of

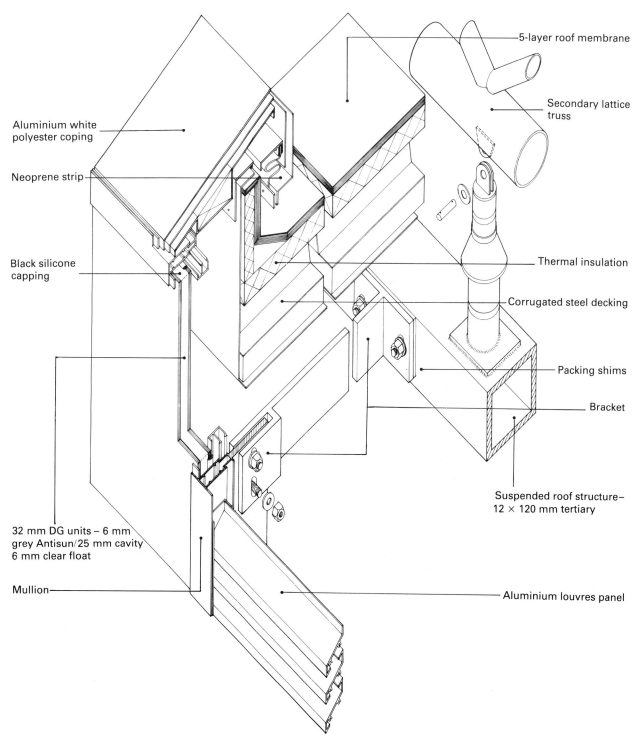

Aluminium white polyester coping

Neoprene strip

Black silicone capping

32 mm DG units – 6 mm grey Antisun/25 mm cavity 6 mm clear float

Mullion

5-layer roof membrane

Secondary lattice truss

Thermal insulation

Corrugated steel decking

Packing shims

Bracket

Suspended roof structure– 12 × 120 mm tertiary

Aluminium louvres panel

Fig. 16.2   Head bracket detail (Courtesy J A Soo)

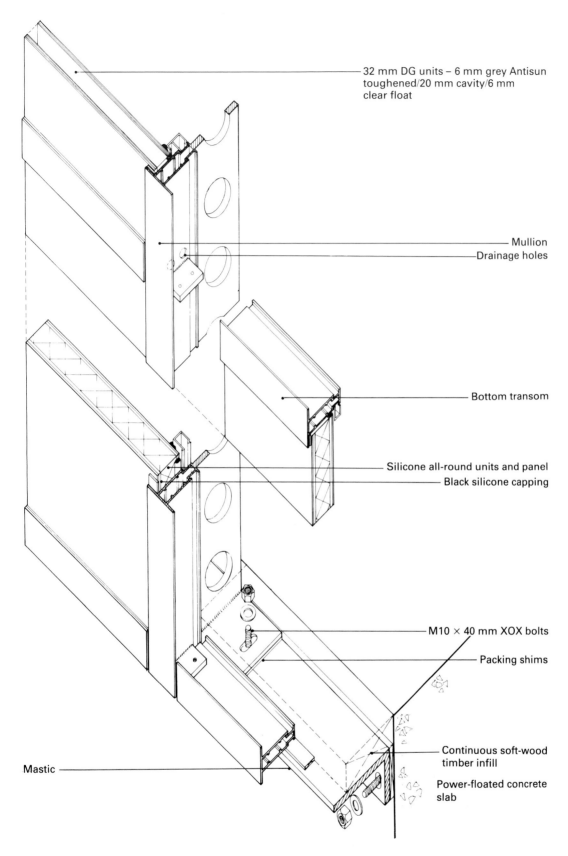

32 mm DG units – 6 mm grey Antisun toughened/20 mm cavity/6 mm clear float

Mullion

Drainage holes

Bottom transom

Silicone all-round units and panel

Black silicone capping

M10 × 40 mm XOX bolts

Packing shims

Continuous soft-wood timber infill

Power-floated concrete slab

Mastic

Fig. 16.3 Mullion, transom and cill detail

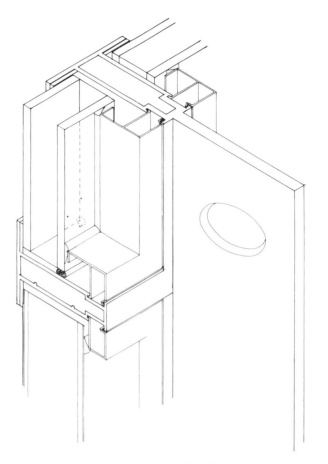

Fig. 16.4   Spine and panel junction (Courtesy of Jane Williams)

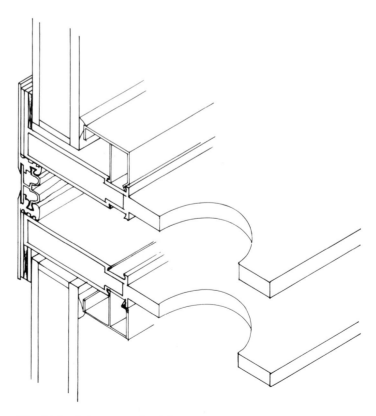

Fig. 16.5   Spine expansion joint

Fig. 16.6   Close-up of panel assembly

6-mm grey 'Antisun', 25-mm cavity and 6-mm clear float. Total thickness 32 mm.

The essential difference between the relative position of perforated mullions to panels used at INMOS and those at the Renault Centre (see case study 21) is that, in this case, the web faces inwards with the glazing bead on the inner face, thus forcing the panels against the projecting outer flange. At Renault, this principle is reversed. The INMOS detail, therefore, puts greater reliance on the silicone outer seal, particularly on the transom members. The resulting strong expression of white horizontal and vertical members, supporting the 1.2 m by 1.2 m panels, contrasts well with the lightweight nature of the exposed structural frame, providing an effective but economical answer to the external skin.

Further reading

1. Ackermann, K (1984)
    'Industriebau' Deutsche Verlags-Anstalt, Stuttgart 1984, 206–13

2. Anon (1982)
    'INMOS moves in: arch. Richard Rogers and Partners', *Building*, Vol. 242, No. 7241, 14 May 1982, 11

3. Hunt, A (1982)
    'AR Detail 1. Structural Details — INMOS micro-computer factory. AR Detail', *Architectural Review*, Dec. 1982

4. Murray, P (1980)
    'Architecture for the microchip era', *RIBA Journal*, Sept. 1980, 45–8

5. Rogers, R (1982)
    'Factory, Newport, Gwent, South Wales — architect's account', *Architectural Review*, Dec. 1982, 26–41

6. Simpson, J (1981)
    'Building an Inmos starship for a technological tomorrow', *Building Design*, No. 575, 18 Dec. 1981, 6

7. Spring, M (1982)
    'Blue chip factory: the INMOS microchip factory in Newport, Gwent', *Building*, Vol. 243, No. 7251, 10 Dec. 1982, 31–4

8. Sudjic, D (1982)
    'Richard Rogers Ltd, fast tracking in Wales', *RIBA Journal*, Jan. 1982, 31–7

Case Study 17 Lloyd's Redevelopment, London

Fig. 17.1 Site under construction

General

Located in the heart of the City of London, this scheme was designed by Richard Rogers and Partners in 1978 as a result of a limited competition. Work is still under construction in 1984. The brief was to design a new building for Lloyd's of London, the insurance underwriters, which would be highly efficient, flexible and respond to their needs for the next fifty years. The result is a large open space on the ground floor to be used as the market area and known as 'the Room'. This will be dominated by a central atrium, which rises the full height of the building, covered by glazed vaulting, which will also light the gallery and floors above.

The rectangular form of the building is layered on each of the eleven floors to break down its profile, while also offering views across the City.

Six satellite towers fill the rest of the site. These towers, containing lifts, toilets and service stairs, also serve to hold the whole building together, both visually and functionally.

Cladding

The service towers are completely clad in stainless-steel insulated panels by Josef Gartner of Germany, who were also responsible for the curtain walling. This triple-glazed system is of unusual design in that it allows surplus warm air, from the interior of the building, to be passed down the outer skin through the cavity between the glazing, thus forming an efficient thermal barrier. Where the glazed opening lights occur, the warm air passes down the mullions. The characteristic stainless-steel 'fishtails' at ground-floor level act as ducts extracting the warm air back into the floor/ceiling zone.

Horizontal adjustment on the cladding is achieved by a split coupled mullion, one side of which is combined with the perforated structure fin. A cranked cast-aluminium bracket with rocker joints at each end forms the link between the mullion heads and the structure. A sliding joint is provided at the frame head and the mullion base support is threaded for adjustability in level.

The service modules, which link into the service towers containing the staircases and toilets, are also made in laminated stainless steel by Jordans of Bristol. Neoprene extrusions are used to take account of variations in level and plan up to ± 20 mm.

The triple glazing to the offices has been specially designed and manufactured for this project. This has a dimpled surface, which reflects light to bring sparkle and life to the exterior walls in the daytime and at night.

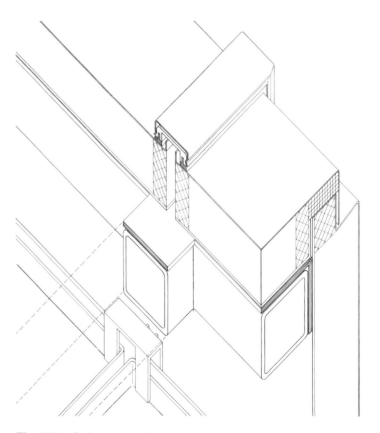

Fig. 17.2 Staircase cladding, wall and roof junction (Courtesy of Rob Loader)

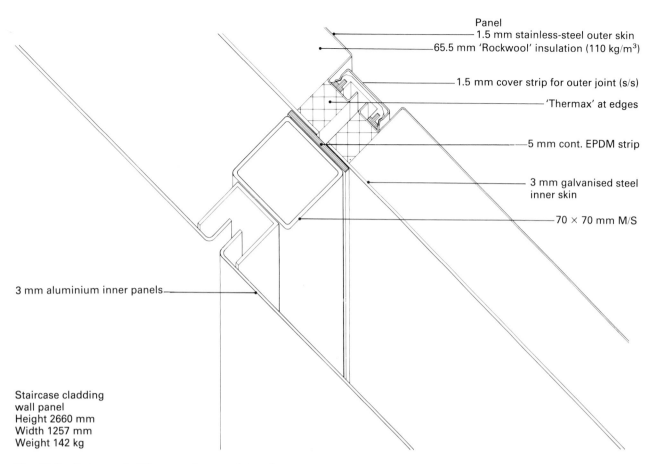

Panel
1.5 mm stainless-steel outer skin
65.5 mm 'Rockwool' insulation (110 kg/m³)

1.5 mm cover strip for outer joint (s/s)

'Thermax' at edges

5 mm cont. EPDM strip

3 mm galvanised steel inner skin

70 × 70 mm M/S

3 mm aluminium inner panels

Staircase cladding
wall panel
Height 2660 mm
Width 1257 mm
Weight 142 kg

Fig. 17.3 Staircase cladding, panel to panel junction

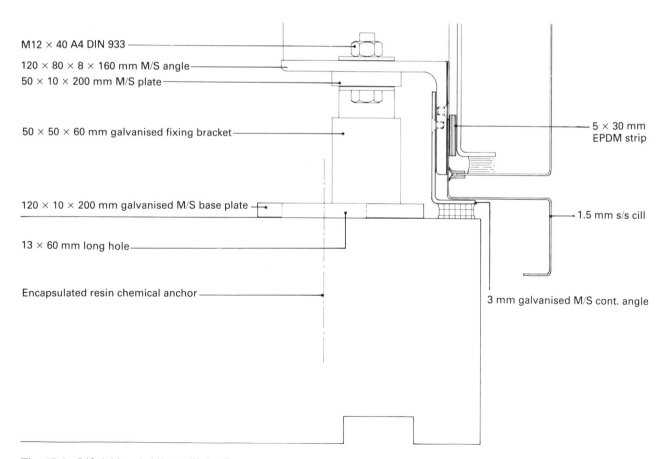

M12 × 40 A4 DIN 933

120 × 80 × 8 × 160 mm M/S angle
50 × 10 × 200 mm M/S plate

50 × 50 × 60 mm galvanised fixing bracket

5 × 30 mm EPDM strip

120 × 10 × 200 mm galvanised M/S base plate

1.5 mm s/s cill

13 × 60 mm long hole

Encapsulated resin chemical anchor

3 mm galvanised M/S cont. angle

Fig. 17.4 Lift lobby cladding, cill detail

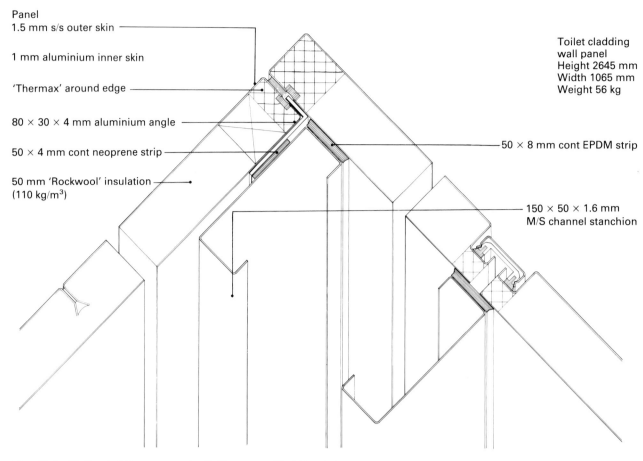

Panel
1.5 mm s/s outer skin

1 mm aluminium inner skin

'Thermax' around edge

80 × 30 × 4 mm aluminium angle

50 × 4 mm cont neoprene strip

50 mm 'Rockwool' insulation
(110 kg/m³)

Toilet cladding
wall panel
Height 2645 mm
Width 1065 mm
Weight 56 kg

50 × 8 mm cont EPDM strip

150 × 50 × 1.6 mm
M/S channel stanchion

Fig. 17.5 Toilet cladding: corner detail (Courtesy of Rob Loader)

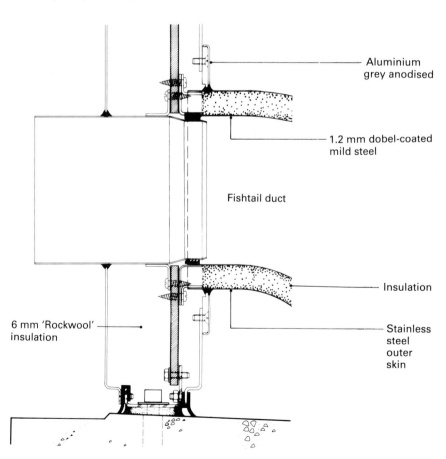

Aluminium
grey anodised

1.2 mm dobel-coated
mild steel

Fishtail duct

Insulation

Stainless
steel
outer
skin

6 mm 'Rockwool'
insulation

Fig. 17.6 Fishtail duct detail (Courtesy of Chris Grech)

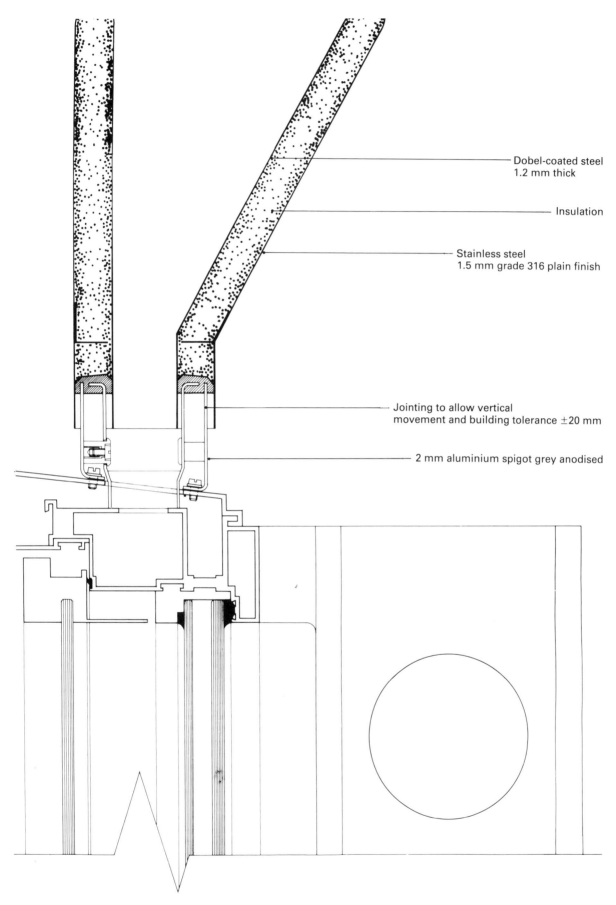

Dobel-coated steel
1.2 mm thick

Insulation

Stainless steel
1.5 mm grade 316 plain finish

Jointing to allow vertical
movement and building tolerance ±20 mm

2 mm aluminium spigot grey anodised

Fig. 17.7 Fishtail duct detail

Further reading

1. Anon (1980)
   'Projekt fur die Lloyd's Versicherer in London', *Bauen & Wohnen*, Vol. 4, 1980, 14–27

2. Cruikshank, D (1981)
   'Lloyd's redevelopment, City of London', *Architectural Review*, May 1981, 26–32

3. Young, J, Rice, P & Thornton, J (1984)
   'Design for better assembly 5 Case Study: Rogers and Arups', *Architects' Journal*, 5 Sept. 1984; Waters, B (1984) 'A year at Lloyd's building', 21 Sept., 31–6

Case Study 18   Milton Keynes Advanced Factory Units, Kiln Farm, Milton Keynes

Fig. 18.1   Overall view of building under construction

General

Developed by the Milton Keynes Development Corporation between 1973 and 1976, the cladding system used on three phases of advanced factory units at Milton Keynes demonstrated one of the first examples of stamped-metal panel systems used in this country. Using techniques evolved by the motor car industry, these panels developed principles of design long promoted by Jean Prouve, as seen in the panels of the French Atomic Energy building at Pierrelatte.

Panels

The 1 m by 2 m panels were stamped out in one operation using CR1 extra deep drawing grade Stelvetite 6 Steel (20 swg thick) and finished in bright yellow plastisol coating. In this way, the rigidity of the panel is achieved by their pressed shape, without need for further stiffening. Plastic-capped screws were used to fix the panels onto a timber batten fixed to 100 mm by 65 mm mild steel angle sheeting rails spanning between 127 mm by 76 mm vertical hot-rolled steel I sections at 2-m centres. Single panels were light enough for one man to handle during assembly.

Internal lining and insulation was provided by 10-mm foil-backed PVC-faced industrial grade plasterboard, supported on timber packing pieces at 1-m centres (U value given as 1.7 W/m²).

Window openings (see Figs 18.1 and 18.2) could be punched out during manufacture or cut at any time after erection. Window glazing was directly mounted into the panel using neoprene gaskets. Horizontal-sliding aluminium windows such as those often seen in buses could also be located in the same size hole using neoprene gaskets.

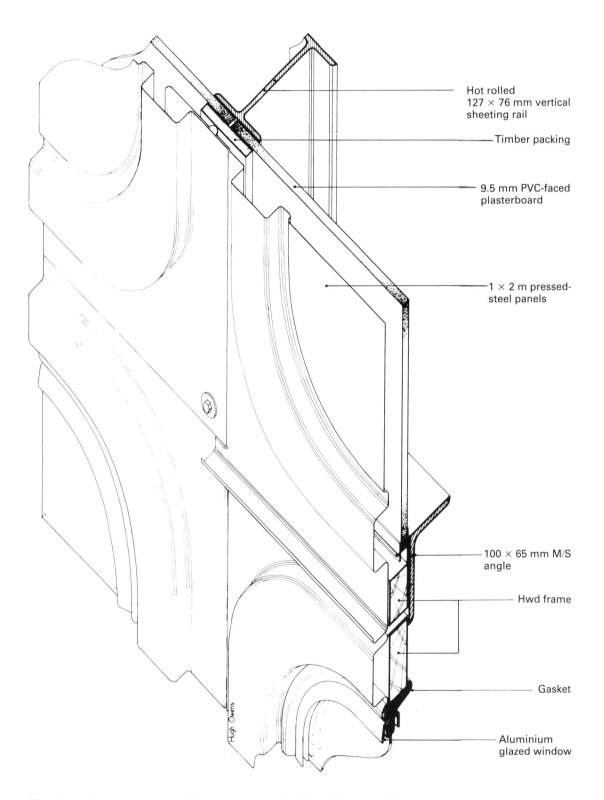

Hot rolled
127 × 76 mm vertical
sheeting rail

Timber packing

9.5 mm PVC-faced
plasterboard

1 × 2 m pressed-
steel panels

100 × 65 mm M/S
angle

Hwd frame

Gasket

Aluminium
glazed window

Fig. 18.2 Panel to panel assembly showing head of window (Courtesy of Hugh Owens)

One of the interesting aspects of the façade is that the personnel doors were made by using similar panels fixed vertically into a timber frame. Vehicle doors 5 m high by 4 m were made by fixing panels to an overhead door frame. The result, while maintaining a consistent façade appearance, makes location of entry points to the building, on what seems an almost endless grid of panels, somewhat difficult.

As the steel panels were overlapped at their edges, like slates, and site fixed to the timber packing pieces, this caused some rather unsightly

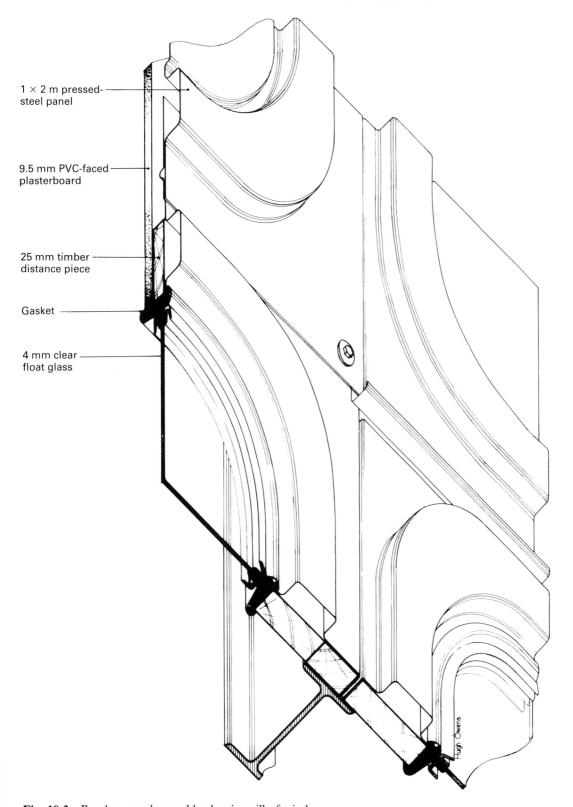

1 × 2 m pressed-steel panel

9.5 mm PVC-faced plasterboard

25 mm timber distance piece

Gasket

4 mm clear float glass

Fig. 18.3 Panel to panel assembly showing cill of window

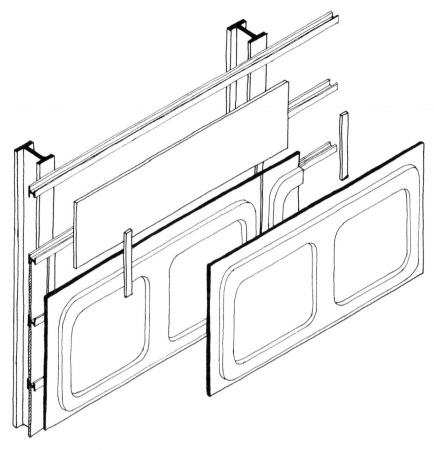

Fig. 18.4 Steel panels mounted on subframes with timber battens

Fig. 18.5 Panels during assembly

Fig. 18.6 Door to panel detail (Photo by John Donat)

Fig. 18.7 Overhead door made with similar panels

detailing problems at the corners of the panels and doors (see Fig. 18.6). Further, the joints are not completely airtight and, according to Drury[3], this gave rise to complaints from the occupants.

Further reading

1. Anon (1976)
   'Advance factory units – Phase 3 – Kiln Farm', *Architects' Journal*, 22 and 29 Dec. 1976

2. Auger, B (1975)
   'Plastics coated steel', *Building*, Vol. 229, No. 42, 17 Oct. 1975, 112–17

3. Drury, J (1981)
   Factories, planning, design and modernisation. Architectural Press, London, 1981, p. 233

4. Hindhaugh, E W (1981)
   'Coated steel in construction industry: present and future uses', *Production and use of coil coated strip*. Metals Society, London, 1981

5. Williams, A (1973)
   'Building dossier factory building', *Building*, Vol. 224, No. 25, 22 June 1973, 87

Case Study 19 Norweb Offices, Ashton-under-Lyne

Fig. 19.1 Organised composition of vitreous-enamelled panels (Photo by Jeremy Preston)

General

This two-storey complex of office buildings and light workshops was designed by architects John Gaytten Associates and completed in 1983 in response to a defined brief from the North West Electricity Board. Working within the discipline of a modular grid of vitreous-enamelled steel cladding panels, the windows and doors have been carefully placed to form an organised composition. This is in contrast to Richard Rogers' INMOS (see case study 16) where the windows and panels were interchangeable in response to future client requirements.

Cladding

Vitreous-enamelled steel panels are limited in size by the availability of the zero carbon steel necessary for their manufacture (see Brookes[1], p. 179). It makes sense, therefore, to mount these panels on a subframe assembly in the factory and to transport them to site as large fabricated units. Escol Limited, the manufacturers of the panels, had already used this principle of design, which incidentally reduces the amount of site jointing, at Burne House in London (see case study 3).

Panels

Thus each of the panels has its own framing system formed of mild-steel channels and rolled hollow sections. The edges of the panels are marked by 102 mm by 51 mm channel painted two-part epoxy blue, which also produces a powerful 'tartan' type grid on the façade where the panels meet.

The 50-mm thick porcelain-enamelled steel insulated panels are fixed back to the subframe with non-ferrous screws through a continuous preformed gasket, acting as a thermal break. The 15-mm joint between the vitreous-enamelled panels consists of 6-mm deep silicone sealant with 25-mm diameter 'Ethafoam' backing strip. Joints between the framed panel units are formed using fircone-shaped neoprene gaskets pressed into the joints between the channels which surround each unit.

The inside face of the cladding is covered with 9-mm marine plywood with joints carefully sealed to form a continuous vapour barrier. In the office areas, an additional interior layer of 12-mm asbestos-free board is provided with a decorative finish.

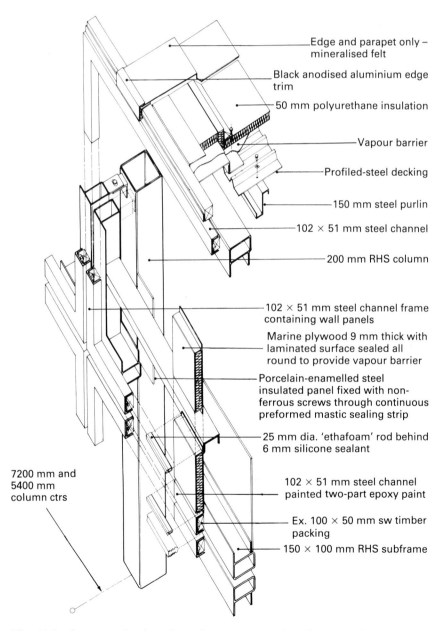

Edge and parapet only – mineralised felt

Black anodised aluminium edge trim

50 mm polyurethane insulation

Vapour barrier

Profiled-steel decking

150 mm steel purlin

102 × 51 mm steel channel

200 mm RHS column

102 × 51 mm steel channel frame containing wall panels

Marine plywood 9 mm thick with laminated surface sealed all round to provide vapour barrier

Porcelain-enamelled steel insulated panel fixed with non-ferrous screws through continuous preformed mastic sealing strip

25 mm dia. 'ethafoam' rod behind 6 mm silicone sealant

102 × 51 mm steel channel painted two-part epoxy paint

Ex. 100 × 50 mm sw timber packing

150 × 100 mm RHS subframe

7200 mm and 5400 mm column ctrs

Fig. 19.2 Axonometric view of panel to panel assembly (Courtesy of Gareth Naylor)

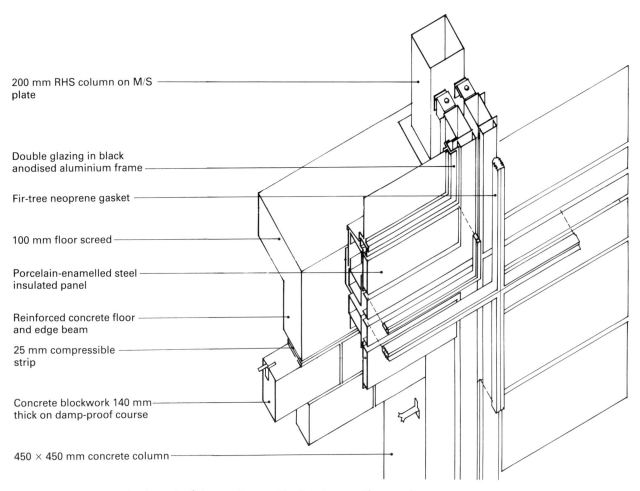

200 mm RHS column on M/S plate

Double glazing in black anodised aluminium frame

Fir-tree neoprene gasket

100 mm floor screed

Porcelain-enamelled steel insulated panel

Reinforced concrete floor and edge beam

25 mm compressible strip

Concrete blockwork 140 mm thick on damp-proof course

450 × 450 mm concrete column

Fig. 19.3 Axonometric view of window wall assembly showing cruciform gasket

Further reading

1. Brookes, A J (1983)
   Cladding of Buildings. Construction Press, London, 1983

2. Winter, J (1983)
   'Skin tests — 2 Electric grid', *Architects' Journal*, 14 Sept. 1983, 76–88

Fig. 20.1 General view showing ribbed steel panels

General

Longton Industrial Holdings (Managing Director Nigel Dale), a large public company with interests in transport and engineering, approached Michael Hopkins Architects in 1980 to develop a high-quality building system, primarily for use as industrial units and office accommodation. The first of these nursery industrial units was erected at their factory at Stoke-on-Trent. The building is supplied as a complete package and, apart from the ground-floor slab, no wet trades are involved. Erection can be carried out by a small team in approximately ten days. Internal dimensions of a typical unit are 18 m long by 12 m wide by 3.85 m high.

Structure

The unique structure designed by Anthony Hunt Associates, Engineers (Project Engineer Mark Whitby), consists of welded tubular portal frame trusses linked by stainless-steel connectors to rectangular hollow-section purlins and angle cross rails, suspended below the lower boom of the trusses. The externally-expressed frame, consisting of a series of centrally-hinged trusses, is so designed that under wind loading compression is developed in the outer boom but only at the knee and in the legs, which are restrained by a single horizontal tubular tie linking the outside of the truss knee joints.

Cladding

The 3.6 m by 1.2 m cladding panels are formed from two skins of 0.8-mm hot-dip galvanised sheet steel, to provide a boxed construction 150 mm thick filled with mineral-wool insulation during manufacture, constructed to prevent cold bridging and to create an impervious inner lining (insulation value of 0.22 W/m^2K). Finish to panels allows for chemical wash to degrease and decontaminate hot-dip galvanised substrate, followed by stoved PVf2 paint system (finish silver grey).

The panels are supported by the 100 mm by 50 mm by 3.2 mm thick rectangular hollow-section purlins with 40 mm by 40 mm by 5 mm thick mild steel angles attached on two sides suspended below and at right angles to the portal frames on 32-mm diameter stainless-steel connectors. The panels thus span across their shorter dimension and are formed with regular troughed indentations to provide rigidity. Structural calculations for the external panels were based on the diaphragm action of the outer skin only, which was Z5 deep drawing steel and profiled to a greater depth than the inner skin, which was Z2 galvanised steel strip.

These indentations are stamped into the flat 0.8-mm sheet by three operations on a deep drawing press. Early prototypes suffered from oil canning after pressing and finishing. However, a small additional indentation at the face of each pressing solved this particular problem.

The four edges of the panels are profiled to interlock with the purlins and the two 40 mm by 40 mm by 5 mm angle cross rails running under the trusses.

End walls were constructed using Forster rolled and welded steel frames (section 0153S and 0253S) welded together as ladders (horizontal sections 60 mm, vertical doubled sections 80 mm).

Jointing

The 'tartan' grid of panels fitting into the purlins and cross rails is sealed using ethylene propylene gaskets, by Climax Building Gaskets, which fit as a continuous frame, with moulded corners, around the edge of each panel. The EPDM jointing strip was asymmetrical in the final design, to allow for greater cover on the panel side than the capping strip side and to allow a distinct silver line to be visible between gaskets. Purlin covers are used to enclose the purlins from the inside. These are filled with 'Alphire' compressed mineral-fibre rigid board, to maintain thermal insulation and fire protection.

Construction

In order for this form of press-in joint gasket system to work, the reader will appreciate that a very high degree of accuracy is required from the assembly. Erection tolerances are quoted as ± 1 mm for the overall dimensions of the building; structural fabrication tolerances as ± 0.5 mm, component tolerances as ± 0.25 mm, and gaskets are manufactured to accommodate tolerances/movement in a range of + 1 mm/- 3 mm.

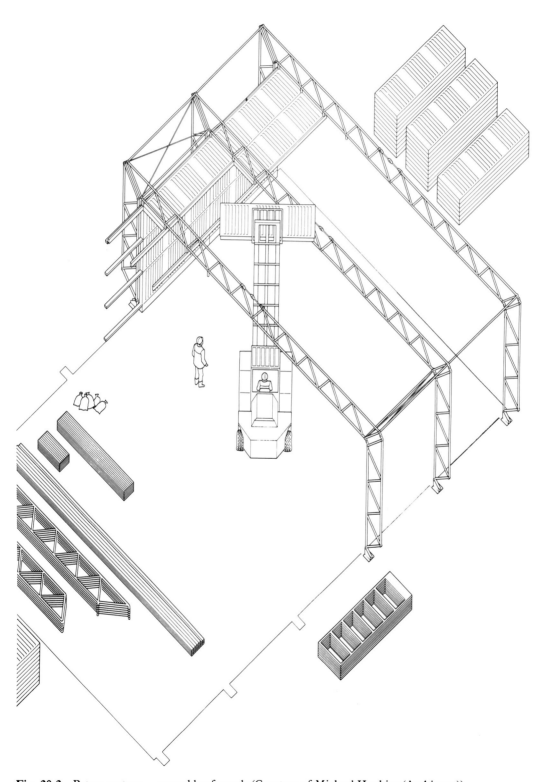

Fig. 20.2 Patera system — assembly of panels (Courtesy of Michael Hopkins (Architects))

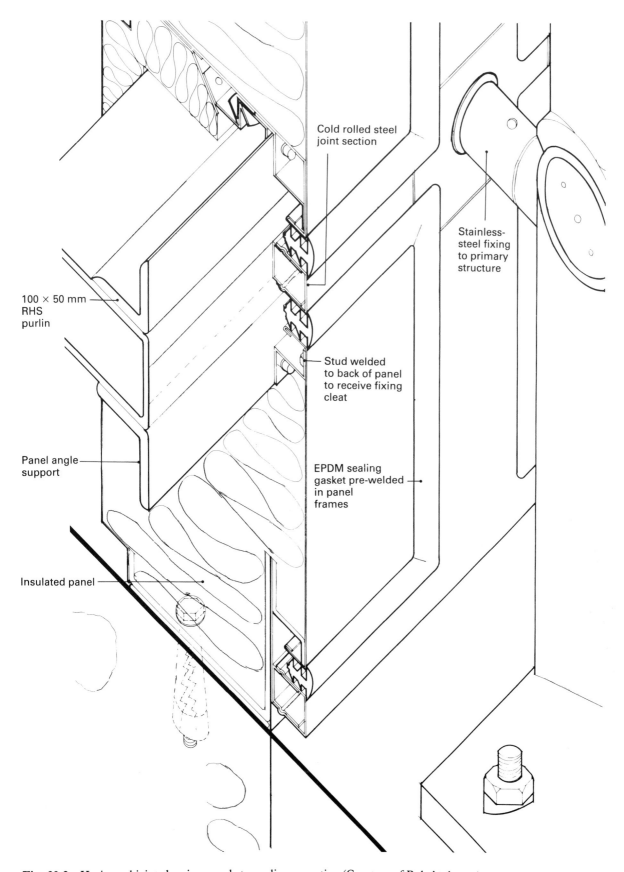

Cold rolled steel
joint section

Stainless-
steel fixing
to primary
structure

100 × 50 mm
RHS
purlin

Stud welded
to back of panel
to receive fixing
cleat

Panel angle
support

EPDM sealing
gasket pre-welded
in panel
frames

Insulated panel

Fig. 20.3 Horizontal joint showing panels to purlin connection (Courtesy of Rob Anderson)

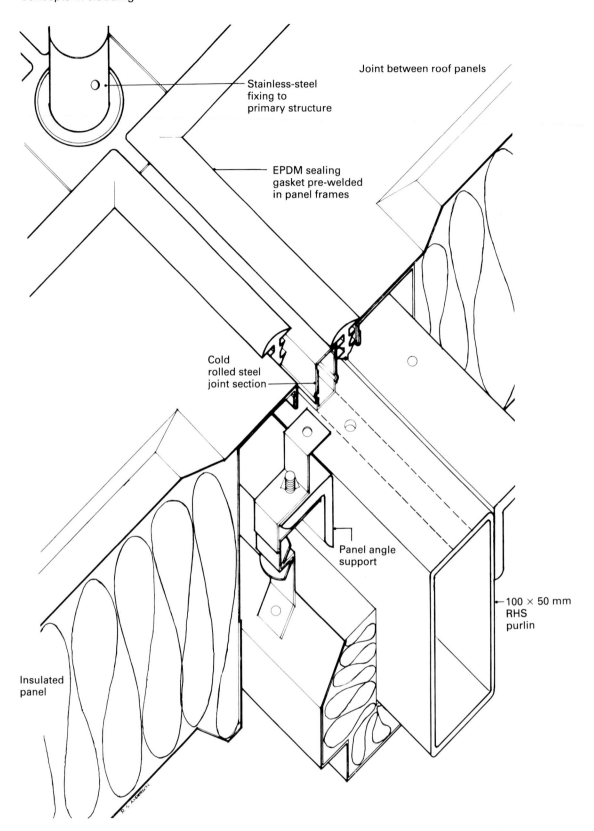

Stainless-steel
fixing to
primary structure

Joint between roof panels

EPDM sealing
gasket pre-welded
in panel frames

Cold
rolled steel
joint section

Panel angle
support

100 × 50 mm
RHS
purlin

Insulated
panel

Fig. 20.4 Joint between roof panels

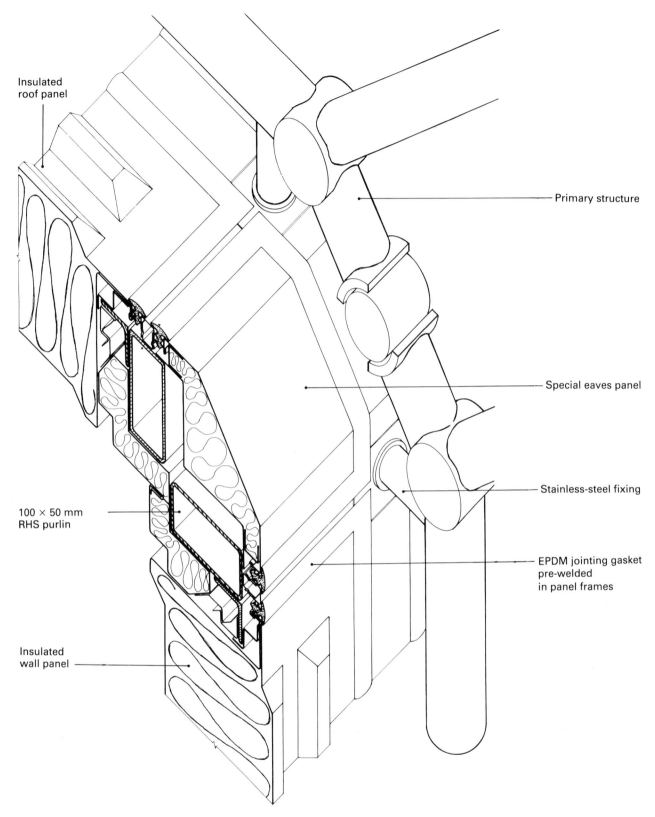

Insulated roof panel

Primary structure

Special eaves panel

Stainless-steel fixing

100 × 50 mm RHS purlin

EPDM jointing gasket pre-welded in panel frames

Insulated wall panel

Fig. 20.5 Eaves detail (Courtesy of K. Anderson)

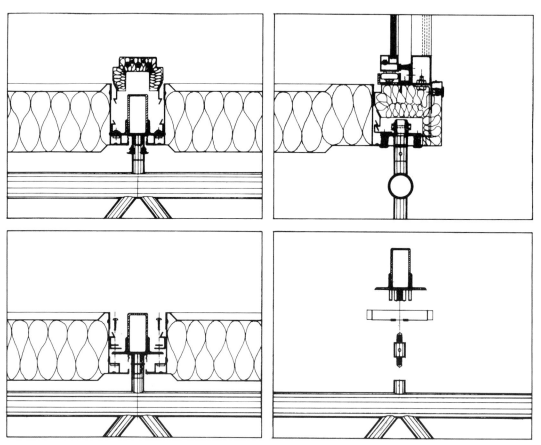

Fig. 20.6 General assembly drawing showing fixing of internal cover piece (Courtesy of Ian Ratcliffe)

Fig. 20.7 Detail fixing to ground slab

Fig. 20.8 Eaves corner piece and exposed structure

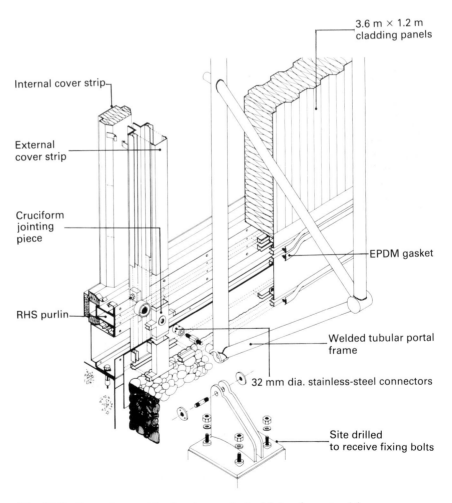

3.6 m × 1.2 m
cladding panels

Internal cover strip

External
cover strip

Cruciform
jointing
piece

EPDM gasket

RHS purlin

Welded tubular portal
frame

32 mm dia. stainless-steel connectors

Site drilled
to receive fixing bolts

Fig. 20.9 General assembly showing method of fixing frame to slab

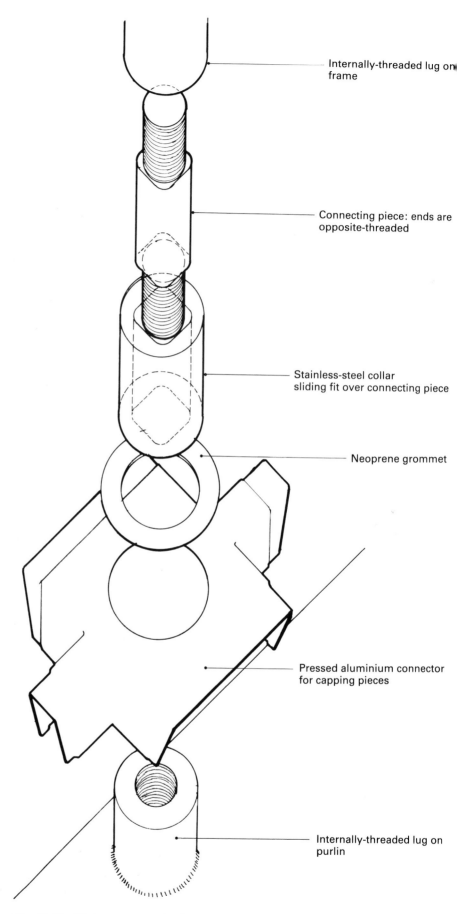

Internally-threaded lug on frame

Connecting piece: ends are opposite-threaded

Stainless-steel collar sliding fit over connecting piece

Neoprene grommet

Pressed aluminium connector for capping pieces

Internally-threaded lug on purlin

Fig. 20.10 Node connector detail

Fig. 20.11 Structure under assembly (Courtesy of *Architects' Journal*; photo by Dave Bower)

In order to obtain these high standards of accuracy, it was necessary to pre-jig the frame and panels in the factory. Trusses were set out in welded jigs and the positions of the stainless-steel connectors accurately located. Purlins were also fabricated to exact lengths and pre-drilled using jigs. These act as a template to co-ordinate the structure and the panels on site and enable fine tolerances to be achieved. Holes for fixing bolts to the anchor plates are drilled with marked positions on site. Pre-positioned anchor bolts are not required.

Further reading

1. Patera Products Ltd (1981)
   The Patera Building. Nov. 1981

2. Patera Products Ltd (1982)
   Patera Buildings. June 1982

3. Whitby, M (1982)
   'Putting paid to Patera puzzle', *Architects' Journal*, 6 Oct. 1982, 53

4. Winter, J (1982)
   'Patera as product', *Architects' Journal*, 1 Sept. 1982, 51–4

5. Worthington, J (1981)
   'Patera as process,' *Architects' Journal*, 1 Sept. 1982, 41–9

Case Study 21   Renault Centre, Swindon, Wiltshire

Fig. 21.1   Overall view of exterior cladding and structural masts (Architects: Foster Associates, photo by Richard Davies)

General

The Renault Centre, designed by architects Foster Associates and engineers Ove Arup and Partners, was built by Bovis under a management contract during 1982 and officially opened in June 1983.

The structure is well known for its forest of bright yellow painted 16-m high tubular masts and tension cables. The building measures 300 m by 108 m on a 6.5-hectare site. Being mainly warehouse, clear spans in both directions were required and the structure is planned in square bays of 24 m by 24 m.

The suspended roof is 7.5 m high at the edge and rises to 9 m at the apex. Ancillary accommodation, comprising mainly offices and showroom, occupies the tapering portion of the site and here the cladding changes from steel composite cladding, as used to clad the warehouse, to a suspended glass assembly.

In essence, the structure is a portal frame with fixed moment connection at the foot of the mast. Arched beams spanning 24 m are supported by ties from the top of the mast at their quarter span and have pre-stressed ties connected to them from the top and bottom of the mast.

The building incorporates many technical innovations but it is the cladding and glazing that concern us here.

Cladding

The main cladding consists of steel panels 3900 mm by 926 mm by 75 mm thick, spanning 4 m between vertical cladding mullions (305 mm by 165 mm by 54 kg/m universal beam).

The panels, manufactured by Tangrose Engineering (now RVP Building Products Ltd) consist of two skins of 0.6-mm steel with 75-mm foamed polyurethane core. The specially designed feature of the panel is the fine profile 0.8 mm deep at 10-mm pitch. This was achieved at surprisingly low cost by using rolling processes developed for other metal products. Panels were finished with PVf2 finish externally and alkyd coating on galvanised steel internally.

Fixing

The panels were fixed at their sides by six 'Buildex' ST+ Type B stainless-steel, 90 mm long, self-tapping fasteners (three each side) back to the rear leg of the universal beam cladding mullion. This cladding mullion was not fixed to the main structure but restrained at its head by a sliding connection. Expansion joints were also included in the assembly using offset fixings.

Jointing

The vertical joint between the panels and the mullions was formed by a U-section neoprene seal glued to both steelwork and panel with silver grey silicone sealant. The horizontal joint between panels consisted of a tongue and groove upstand formed within the top edge preformed edging strip.

At the head of the panel is a 350-mm deep black neoprene gasket, loosely fitting between the top of the panels and the roof edge section. This flexibility is essential to permit three-dimensional movement, thermal or wind generated, between roof and wall ($\pm$ 75 mm vertically, $\pm$ 30 mm horizontally in both directions). In order to prevent flapping of the neoprene, stainless-steel coil springs are stretched vertically down the gasket to the steel section topping the wall; a technique suggested by fabric-sided lorry design. The same detail is used over the glazed office block.

Suspended glazing

Although Pilkington were also responsble for the development of the suspended glazing used at Willis Faber and Dumas (see case study 29), the system developed by them for the Renault Centre is a complete departure from the previous use of metal patches to support the glass. Here, the 4.2-m long by 1.8-m high sheets of Armourplate glass are held in place by eight 6-mm bolts connecting the glazing to steel transoms, which in turn transfer the wind loads to the main structural framing. The connection is achieved by means of a steel spring plate member in the form of a 'spider', allowing movement in the plane of the glass.

This system of supporting the glazing has now been patented by Pilkington as their 'Planar' glazing system. The same construction is used at Renault Centre in the twenty-seven trapezoidal rooflights, which give light and outside views to the warehouse, mezzanine offices and showroom.

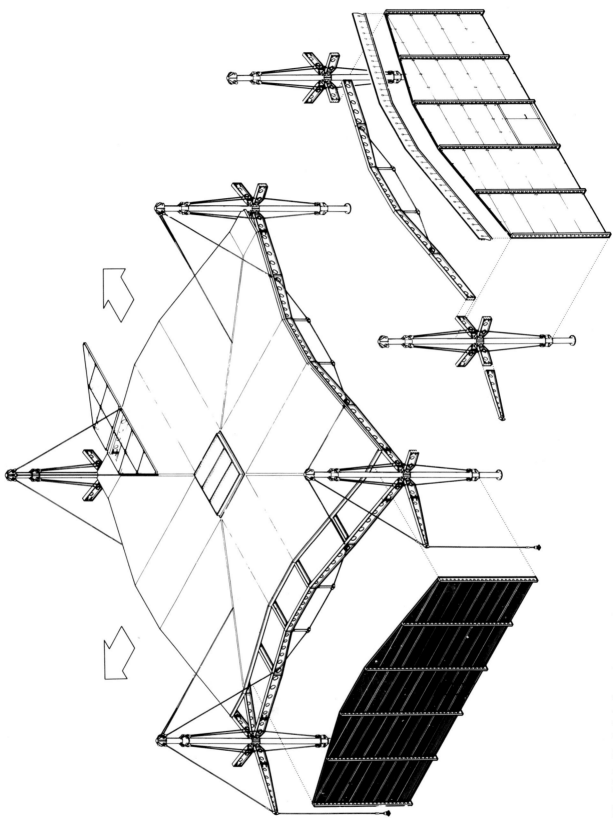

Fig. 21.2 Exploded view of construction showing arched beams (Courtesy of Foster Associates)

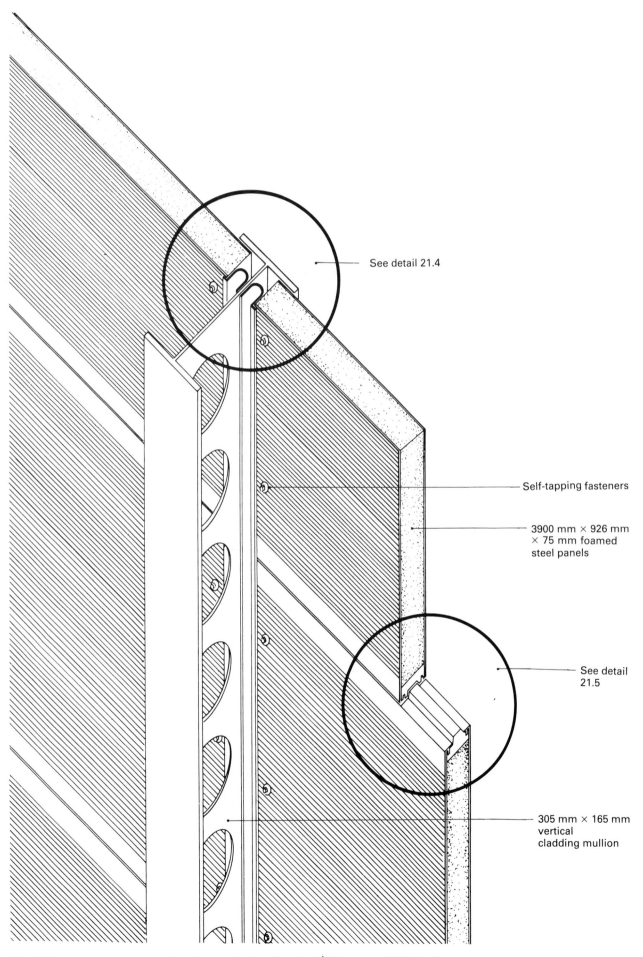

See detail 21.4

Self-tapping fasteners

3900 mm × 926 mm
× 75 mm foamed
steel panels

See detail
21.5

305 mm × 165 mm
vertical
cladding mullion

Fig. 21.3 Axonometric view of panel to vertical mullion detail (Courtesy of RVP Ltd).

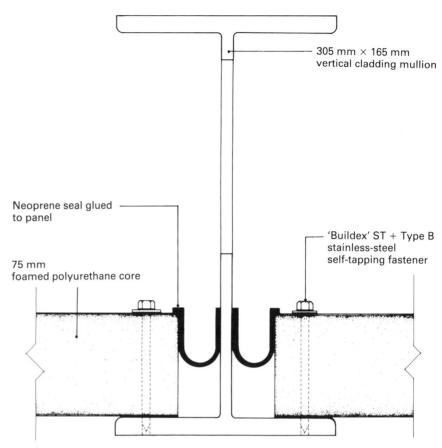

Fig. 21.4 Plan of panel to vertical mullion (Courtesy of RVP Ltd)

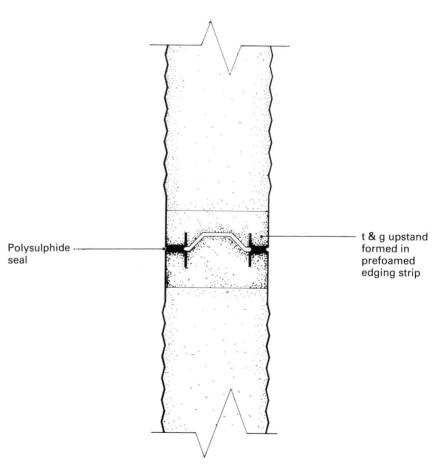

Fig. 21.5 Section through horizontal joint between panels

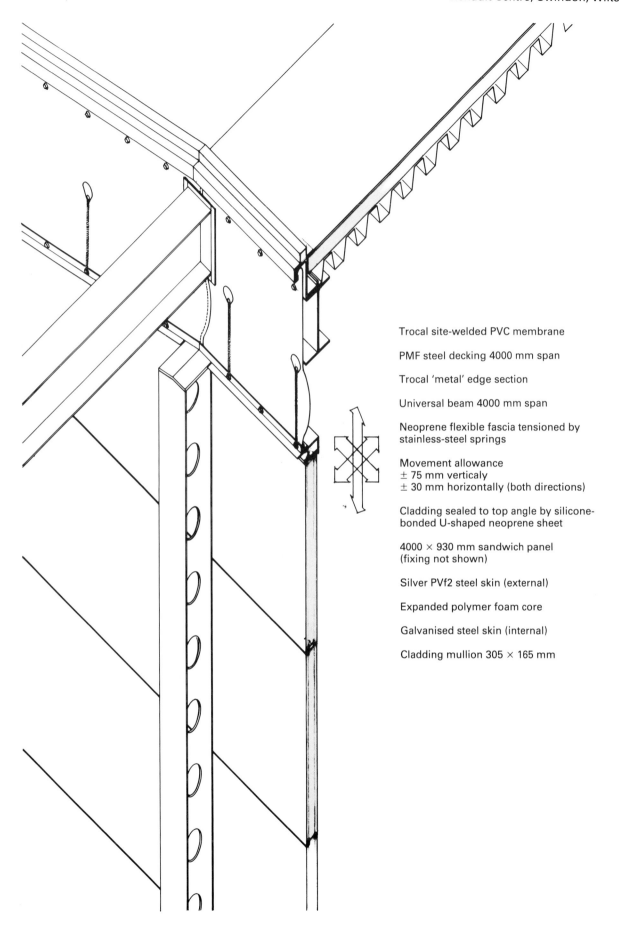

Trocal site-welded PVC membrane

PMF steel decking 4000 mm span

Trocal 'metal' edge section

Universal beam 4000 mm span

Neoprene flexible fascia tensioned by
stainless-steel springs

Movement allowance
± 75 mm verticaly
± 30 mm horizontally (both directions)

Cladding sealed to top angle by silicone-
bonded U-shaped neoprene sheet

4000 × 930 mm sandwich panel
(fixing not shown)

Silver PVf2 steel skin (external)

Expanded polymer foam core

Galvanised steel skin (internal)

Cladding mullion 305 × 165 mm

Fig. 21.6 Axonometric view of wall to roof junction (Courtesy of Mike Stacey)

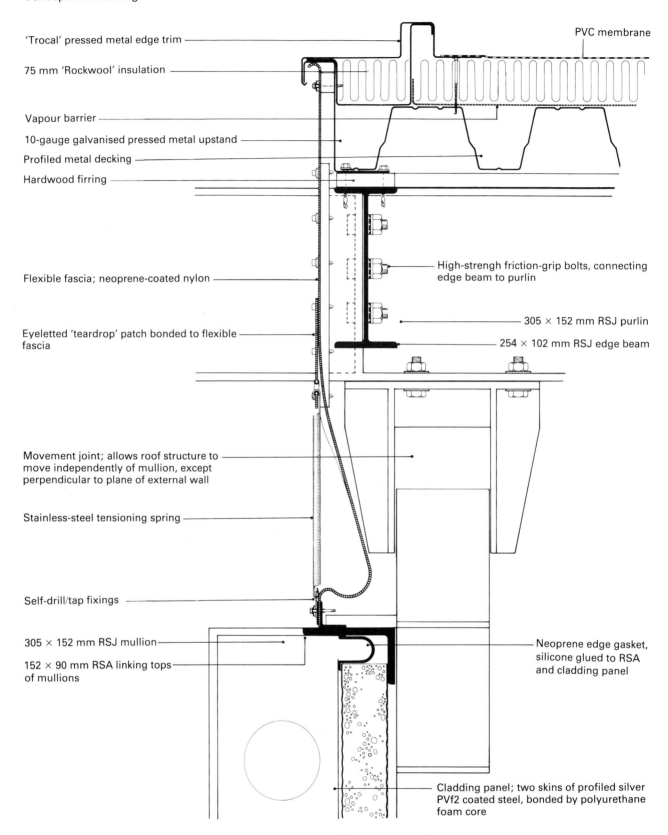

'Trocal' pressed metal edge trim

PVC membrane

75 mm 'Rockwool' insulation

Vapour barrier

10-gauge galvanised pressed metal upstand

Profiled metal decking

Hardwood firring

High-strengh friction-grip bolts, connecting edge beam to purlin

Flexible fascia; neoprene-coated nylon

305 × 152 mm RSJ purlin

Eyeletted 'teardrop' patch bonded to flexible fascia

254 × 102 mm RSJ edge beam

Movement joint; allows roof structure to move independently of mullion, except perpendicular to plane of external wall

Stainless-steel tensioning spring

Self-drill/tap fixings

305 × 152 mm RSJ mullion

152 × 90 mm RSA linking tops of mullions

Neoprene edge gasket, silicone glued to RSA and cladding panel

Cladding panel; two skins of profiled silver PVf2 coated steel, bonded by polyurethane foam core

Fig. 21.7 Section through wall to roof junction (Courtesy of Foster Associates)

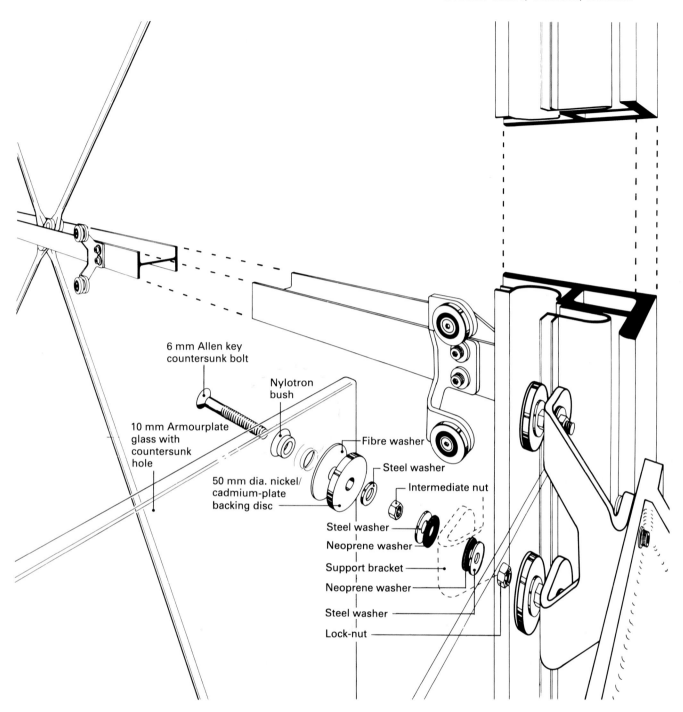

6 mm Allen key
countersunk bolt

Nylotron
bush

10 mm Armourplate
glass with
countersunk
hole

50 mm dia. nickel/
cadmium-plate
backing disc

Fibre washer

Steel washer

Intermediate nut

Steel washer

Neoprene washer

Support bracket

Neoprene washer

Steel washer

Lock-nut

Fig. 21.8 Detail of the 'Planar' glazing system at internal angle between
showroom and cafeteria (Courtesy of Foster Associates)

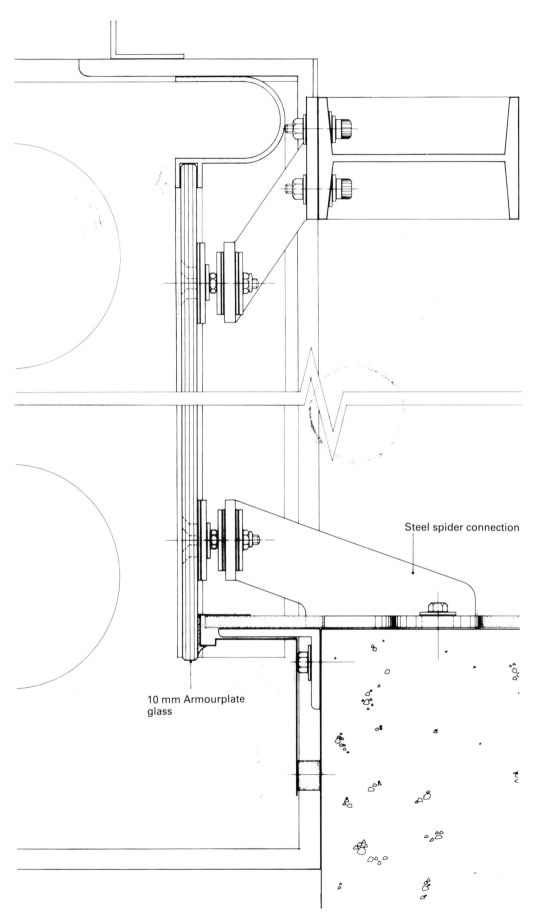

Steel spider connection

10 mm Armourplate
glass

Fig. 21.9 Section through glazing showing steel spider connection

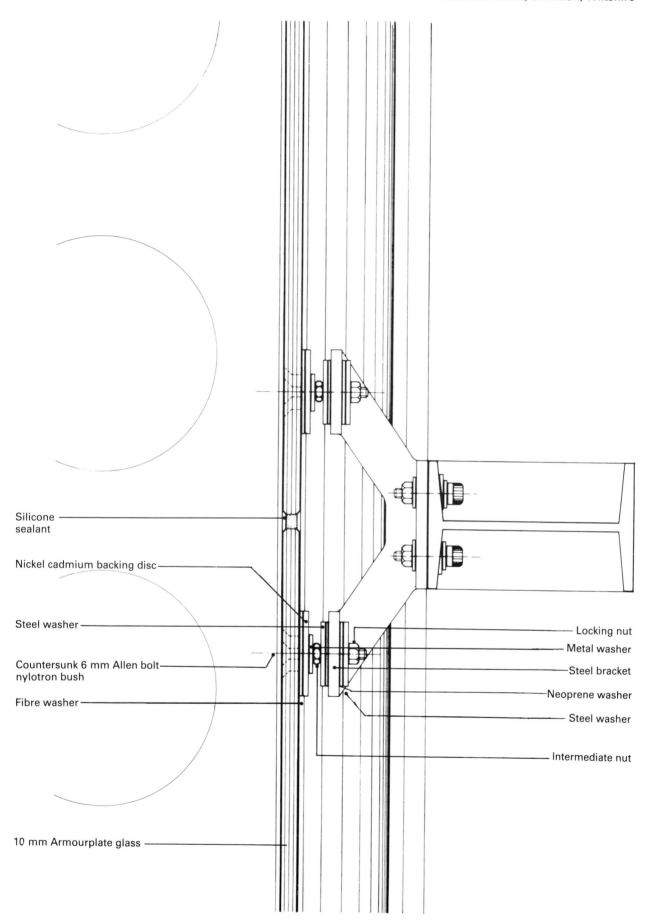

Silicone sealant

Nickel cadmium backing disc

Steel washer

Countersunk 6 mm Allen bolt nylotron bush

Fibre washer

Locking nut

Metal washer

Steel bracket

Neoprene washer

Steel washer

Intermediate nut

10 mm Armourplate glass

Fig. 21.10 Horizontal joint between glazing (Courtesy of Chris Grech)

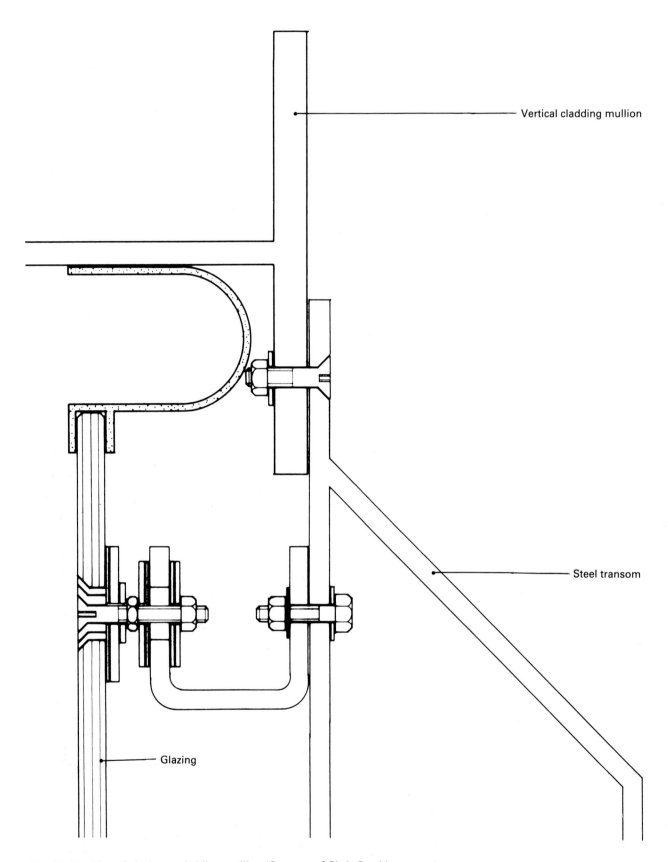

Vertical cladding mullion

Steel transom

Glazing

Fig. 21.11 Plan of glazing to cladding mullion (Courtesy of Chris Grech)

Fig. 21.12 Side view of panels showing profile (Photo by Richard Parker)

Fig. 21.13 Glazing to offices and showroom

Fig. 21.14   Steel spider connection viewed from inside (Photo by Chris Grech)

Fig. 21.15   Base of glazing

Fig. 21.16 Close-up of panel profile (Courtesy of RVP Ltd)

Further reading

1. Anon (1982)
   'Renault's umbrella over the Swindon skyline', *Building Design*, 3 Sept. 1982

2. Best, A (1982)
   'Foster at play', *Architects' Journal*, 1 Dec. 1982, 40–1

3. Davey, P (1983)
   'Renault Centre, Swindon, Wiltshire,' *Architectural Review*, July 1983, 20–32

4. Matthews, R (1983)
   'Glass by Foster', *Building*, 18 Mar. 1983, 72–4

5. Newton, P & Burdon, P A (1982)
   Short term load testing of cladding panels for Tangrose Engineering. Teesside Polytechnic, Department of Civil and Structural Engineering, April 1982. Available from RVP Building Products Ltd, Liverpool

6. Pawley, M (1982)
   'If you ever plan to motor west', *Building Design*, 26 Nov. 1982

7. Pawley, M (1983)
   'Renault inspection', *Architects' Journal*, 15 June 1983, 40–5

8. Waters, B (1982)
   'Framework for Renault', *Building*, 22 Oct. 1982, 32–40

Case Study 22 Sainsbury Centre for the Visual Arts, Norwich

Fig. 22.1 Glazed end showing tubular steel truss (Courtesy of John Donat)

General

The Sainsbury Centre for Visual Arts (architects: Foster Associates) was built in 1977 at the University of East Anglia, Norwich, to house the Sainsbury collection of art. The dramatic structure consists of thirty-seven welded tubular prismatic steel trusses spanning 35 m, supported on similar lattice towers creating a column-free interior 133 m in length. A clear height of 7.5 m permits the display of large works of art and the insertion of independent mezzanines.

Cladding

This project gave the opportunity for one of the first commercial applications of superplastic aluminium in building. A consortia of manufacturers, including Modern Art Glass, Leyland and Birmingham Rubber Company and Aluminium Systems of Dublin (Sean Billinge), were guided by the cladding consultant Tony Pritchard into using a new aluminium alloy available from Superform Metals Limited of Worcester, which at that time was a subsidiary of British Aluminium Company Limited.

Presses had been developed to allow panels up to 1.8 m by 1.2 m to be formed with upstand edges up to 100 mm deep using superplastic forming techniques. In this way, it was possible to stretch aluminium at high temperatures with compressed air presses on simple low-cost tools (cost in

1977 for the tool used for Sainsbury Centre panels was approximately £5000).

At that time, alloys with copper additives allowed better stretching capabilities and, because of the comparatively low corrosion environment in Norwich, it was possible to use this alloy as a core with skins of less superplastic but more durable aluminium. Total thickness of the metal was approximately 1.5 mm. Later developments of superplastic aluminium led to Supral 5000, which has a zirconium additive, as used at Aztec West (see case study 1).

The moulded outer skin was finished in natural anodised aluminium. The inner skin, also in aluminium, was pushed into the outer trays and pop riveted with a thermal break between the two metal skins. The box thus formed was filled with 100 mm Phenelux foam sheet cut to receive the aluminium fixing channels. The outer profiles were filled with polystyrene pieces giving a total U value of 0.47 $W/m^2°C$ across the panel.

Glazed panels were formed using an aluminium section into which the glass was filled using a neoprene gasket. The unit has a superplastic aluminium skin around its edges, cut from the insulated panel pressing, with a jointing profile to match that of the solid panels. An extruded aluminium Z-section pre-formed into panel-sized rectangular frames acts as a subframe to support both glazing and panel types. These subframes were bolted to lugs welded to the steel trusses. The panels were fitted to the subframe using six stainless-steel screws.

Jointing

The unique jointing system, using an aluminium carrier system and neoprene gutter section gasket, is used on both walls and roof. This allows a variety of different panel, glazing and louvres assembly, all interchangeable within the carrier system. Total cost of the curtain wall assembly in 1977 was approximately £160 per square metre.

Each panel was fitted into a continuous net of neoprene gaskets by Leyland and Birmingham Rubber Company, fabricated by jointing successive fourteen-panel modules together on site as a lattice work (embracing three modules wide by eight modules long). The four-way junctions were manufactured in the factory and pieces of the net were vulcanised together on site by Modern Art Glass Company Limited at their mid-points prior to fitting the panels using portable equipment. The result is a one-piece gasket weighing more than 12 000 kg which spans the entire roof and walls of the building. The gasket serves a double function in that it acts as a rainwater drainage system in addition to its more usual task of weather sealing. The same panel and gasketing system is used throughout the building envelope for both roof and wall, apart from the glazed end walls. The size of the gutter gasket was influenced by the volume of water being drained from the adjacent panels in relation to the pitch of the roof (350 mm higher at pitch than eaves). This method of assembling joints in gaskets as an integral net throughout a building has been patented by the Leyland and Birmingham Rubber Company.

Glazed end walls

Clear glass walls at east and west ends are 30 m by 7.5 m high. Each sheet of glass (7.5 m by 2.4 m) and its supporting glass fin is supported and restrained by purpose-made steel channels anchored into the floor slab. Glass sheets are joined with high-grade silicone sealant.

Fig. 22.2 Side view of panels showing profile (Photo by Steve Haughton)

Fig. 22.3 Lattice gaskets in place prior to fitting of panels (Courtesy of Leyland & Birmingham Rubber Co Ltd)

Fig. 22.4 Fitting of aluminium panels on to subframe (Courtesy of Superform Metals Ltd)

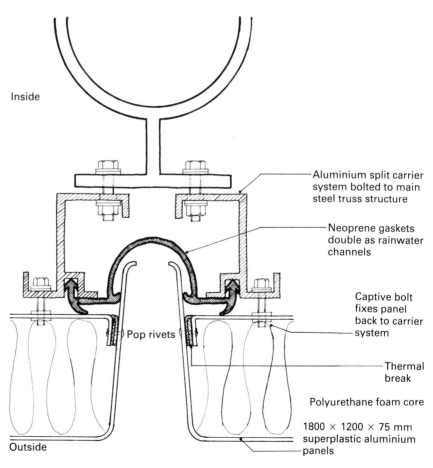

Inside

Aluminium split carrier system bolted to main steel truss structure

Neoprene gaskets double as rainwater channels

Captive bolt fixes panel back to carrier system

Pop rivets

Thermal break

Polyurethane foam core

1800 × 1200 × 75 mm superplastic aluminium panels

Outside

Fig. 22.5 Plan of joint

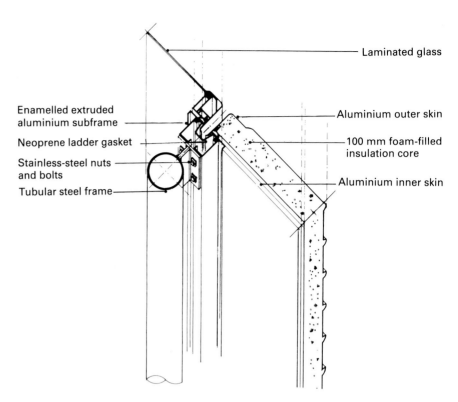

Laminated glass

Enamelled extruded aluminium subframe

Neoprene ladder gasket

Stainless-steel nuts and bolts

Tubular steel frame

Aluminium outer skin

100 mm foam-filled insulation core

Aluminium inner skin

Fig. 22.6 Axonometric view of vertical and horizontal joint (Courtesy of Foon Chow)

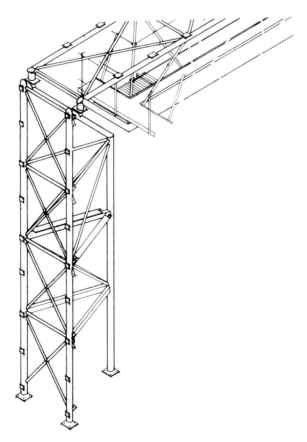

Fig. 22.7 Tubular steel truss

Further reading

1. Anon (1979)
   'Modernised reconstituted', *Progressive Architecture*, Feb. 1979, 49–57

2. Brookes, A J & Ward, M (1981)
   'The art of construction metal claddings — box panels: Sainsbury Centre', *Architects' Journal*, 15 July 1981, 122–3

3. Cook, P (1978)
   'Sainsbury Centre for the Visual Arts', *Architectural Review*, Vol. 164, No. 82, Dec. 1978, 345–62

4. Foster, M (1982)
   The principles of architecture, style, structure and design. Phaidon Press, Oxford, 1982, pp 122–3

5. Leyland and Birmingham Rubber Company Limited
   'Panoply of Panels — current uses of Du Pont elastomers in product design and maintenance', *Elastomers Notebook*, No. 207, Apr. 1979, 663–4

6. Matthews, R (1983)
   'Glass by Foster', *Building*, 18 Mar. 1983, 72–4

7. Peckham, A (1979)
   'Foster Associates Sainsbury Centre', *Architectural Design*, Profile 19, Vol. 49, No. 2, 1979

8. Spring, M (1978)
   'Art shed', *Building*, Vol. 234, No. 7031, 7 Apr. 1978, 52–3

Case Study 23 Schreiber House, Chester

Fig. 23.1 View of veranda showing overhanging roof

General

This house, built in the grounds of an eighteenth-century mansion near Chester and designed by the architect James Gowan, was hailed by the *Architects' Journal* in 1983 as an example of a 'meticulous and concerned approach to the detailed execution of the architect's work' and, as such, has been included in this collection of case studies.

It is an interesting example of the integration of steel columns into the external masonry walls with careful detailing of the window wall junctions. Unfortunately, the house is sited in an undramatic landscape on an estate of houses of rather mediocre design.

Built for the Schreiber family, most of the accommodation is on the ground floor with a self-contained guest suite within the roof space. The overall impression is of a great oversailing roof, apparently floating on the masonry walls below.

Construction

The impression of the roof (Fig. 23.1), built in traditional construction using Port Madoc slates, hovering over the brick external walls (Butterley hand-made Sandringham red bricks) is maintained by the strip of windows and ventilators along the top of the walls. These walls, with their deep reveals and wide cills, appear to have strength more than adequate to support the roof, which is in reality supported by the eight modest circular columns. It is this inter-relationship between the wall and the columns which concerns us here and can compared with similar detailing by Mario Botta in Switzerland with such careful detailing of specially-cut brick piers adjacent to the main entrance doorway and the excellent standard of carpentry, particularly in interior fittings. Even so, the building is disappointing mainly for its context on the site but also for the shape and size of some of the rooms. Also, rather unfortunately, considering such careful detailing, the lead flashings were leaching on to the Port Madoc slates during a visit to the site in 1984.

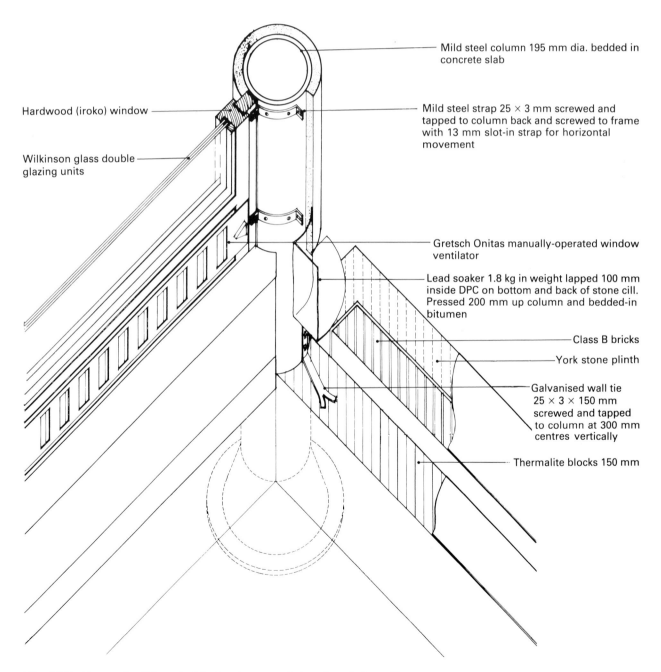

Mild steel column 195 mm dia. bedded in concrete slab

Hardwood (iroko) window

Mild steel strap 25 × 3 mm screwed and tapped to column back and screwed to frame with 13 mm slot-in strap for horizontal movement

Wilkinson glass double glazing units

Gretsch Onitas manually-operated window ventilator

Lead soaker 1.8 kg in weight lapped 100 mm inside DPC on bottom and back of stone cill. Pressed 200 mm up column and bedded-in bitumen

Class B bricks

York stone plinth

Galvanised wall tie 25 × 3 × 150 mm screwed and tapped to column at 300 mm centres vertically

Thermalite blocks 150 mm

Fig. 23.2 Corner detail from inside showing strap fixings for windows (Courtesy of A McCrickard)

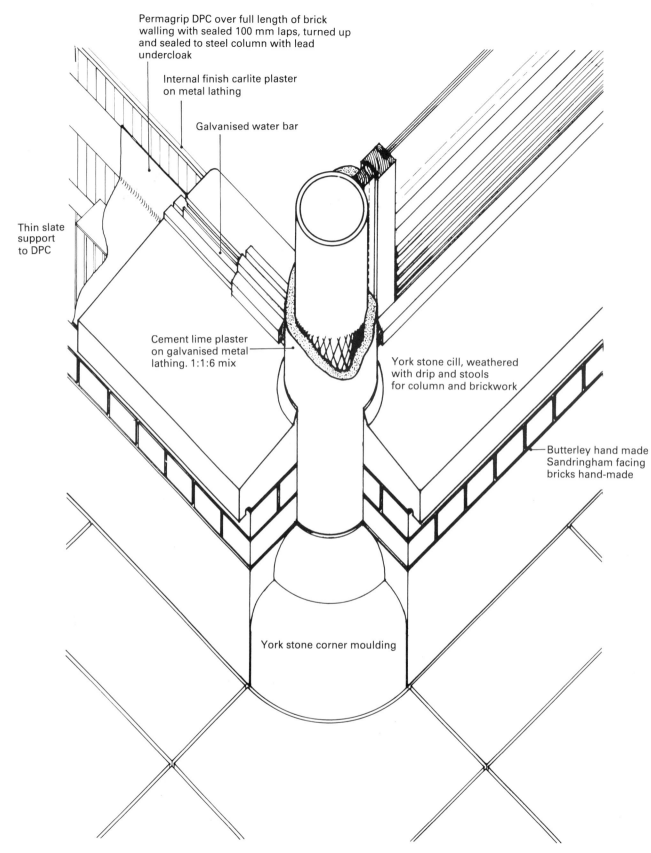

Permagrip DPC over full length of brick
walling with sealed 100 mm laps, turned up
and sealed to steel column with lead
undercloak

Internal finish carlite plaster
on metal lathing

Galvanised water bar

Thin slate
support
to DPC

Cement lime plaster
on galvanised metal
lathing. 1:1:6 mix

York stone cill, weathered
with drip and stools
for column and brickwork

Butterley hand made
Sandringham facing
bricks hand-made

York stone corner moulding

Fig. 23.3 Axonometric showing York stone cill at junction with exterior column

Fig. 23.4 Integration of column with external wall

Further reading

1. Gray, D (1983)
   'Details of a meticulous man', *Architects' Journal*, 26 Jan. 1983, 34–45

2. Nicolin, P & Chaslin, F (1982)
   Mario Botta 1978–1982. Laboratoire d'architecture, Electa Moniteur, Paris, 1982

3. Buchanan, P (1983)
   'Gowan in Chester', *Architectural Review*, Feb. 1983, 39–41

Case Study 24 Schreiber Furniture Factory, Runcorn

Fig. 24.1 General view of Schreiber Factory (Courtesy of Architectural Press)

General

In 1978, Schreiber Furniture Ltd commissioned architects Brock Carmichael Associates to complete their new factory on the Astmoor Industrial Estate in Runcorn New Town.

The rectangular form of the factory follows the linear production process it houses, which is the manufacture of domestic furniture from chipboard and other materials to finished item. Ancillary areas are contained in a linear-storey element on the north wall, and restaurant and conference areas are situated above the despatch bays on the south elevation.

The roof structure consists of triangulated lattice girders spanning 30 m with the top beams equally spaced at 3.75-m centres. The 85-mm deep profiled roof deck (by Briggs Amasco) then spans between these top booms without the need for purlins. Pairs of orange-painted external steel stanchions pick up alternate trusses. Services run through the 2-m deep space provided by the trusses without encroaching on headroom.

Cladding

The external cladding consists of Briggs Amasco colorclad roll-formed profiled steel 35 mm deep on 136 mm by 102 mm by 8 mm sheeting rails at 1-m centres spanning between 254 by 152-mm rolled hollow sections, sheeting posts at 3.75-m centres.

The profiled sheeting is finished in black PVC Plastisol coating. The colours of external orange-painted steelwork and black steel cladding were chosen in accord with Runcorn Development Corporation's overall policy for external treatment of all buildings on the Astmoor Estate.

The 60-mm mineral-wool insulation was stapled to the back face of the 'Supalux' inner lining, which consists of 6-mm insulation board screwed to 38 mm by 32 mm pressed-metal tee sections.

The sloping glazing between the top of the external cladding and the roof edge beam follows the line of the tubular lattice girders. In some respects, this is similar to the glazed roof-edge detail used at Bespak Factory, King's Lynn (see case study 2).

The sloped glazing is formed using Heywood Williams' patent glazing system with an aluminium carrier bar and 6-mm mild steel flat bar (overall 49-mm face width and 86-mm depth) at 65-mm centres. These are cleated to the top and bottom rails with slotted holes to allow expansion and have black anodised finish. The glazing is 6-mm grey Antisun glass.

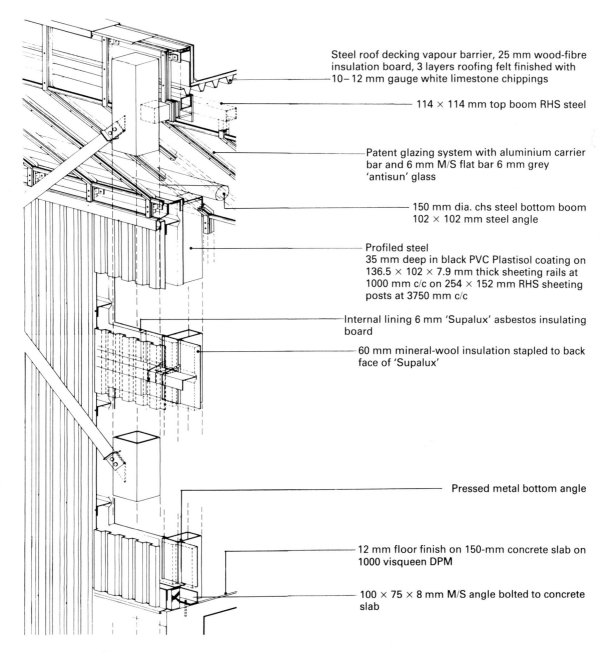

Steel roof decking vapour barrier, 25 mm wood-fibre insulation board, 3 layers roofing felt finished with 10–12 mm gauge white limestone chippings

114 × 114 mm top boom RHS steel

Patent glazing system with aluminium carrier bar and 6 mm M/S flat bar 6 mm grey 'antisun' glass

150 mm dia. chs steel bottom boom 102 × 102 mm steel angle

Profiled steel 35 mm deep in black PVC Plastisol coating on 136.5 × 102 × 7.9 mm thick sheeting rails at 1000 mm c/c on 254 × 152 mm RHS sheeting posts at 3750 mm c/c

Internal lining 6 mm 'Supalux' asbestos insulating board

60 mm mineral-wool insulation stapled to back face of 'Supalux'

Pressed metal bottom angle

12 mm floor finish on 150-mm concrete slab on 1000 visqueen DPM

100 × 75 × 8 mm M/S angle bolted to concrete slab

Fig. 24.2 Profiled steel cladding on cladding rails (Courtesy of S C Chen)

Fig. 24.3 Detail of tubular truss at edge of glazing (Photo by S C Chen)

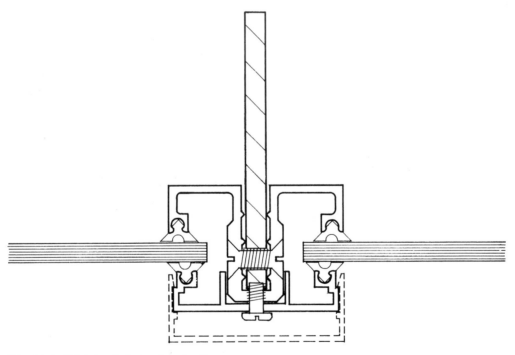

Fig. 24.4 High-level glazing bar detail

Further reading

1. Gale, A (1980)
    'Schreiber Furniture Factory, Runcorn', *Architects' Journal*, 26 Nov. 1980, 1033–51

Case Study 25 South Poplar Health Centre, London

Fig. 25.1 View of building showing modular panels (Courtesy of Henk Snoek Photography & Associates)

General

While the brief for South Poplar was being developed, the architects, Derek Stowe and Partners, were asked by the Department of Health to explore the potential of mass production and by designing the building as a series of capsules which could be assembled in Saudi Arabia. The Saudi project fell through in 1977 but the design, based on a series of modules 3.3 m by 6.6 m by 3.3 m high, was used for a small health centre in South Poplar, London, completed in 1981.

Cladding

The steel panels by Fabcol Ltd (no longer in business), finished with red 'Syntha Pulvin' polyester-powder coating, were mounted in a variant of the standard 'Astrawall' aluminium curtain wall section, which was fixed to hardwood sections on the softwood infill panels, which span from floor to roof steelwork.

The recessed black joint between the panels was formed using the neoprene jointing sections associated with the patent 'Astrawall' curtain wall detail, which also incorporated a 'zipper' gasket.

A feature of the building is the contrast between the deeply-recessed joints between the panels and the thin line of frameless opening windows made in toughened glass which close tightly against the proprietary gasket.

The building has been designed to be relocatable and the windows and cladding are interchangeable, though making a new window or moving one involves repositioning of the studwork behind the panels.

The cost of the external wall and windows is given in the *Architects' Journal*, 18 February 1981, as: 'Enamelled steel panels in neoprene gaskets on aluminium bearers as external cladding including armoured glass windows all on insulated timber studding and lined with fire resistant insulation board finished with emulsion paint — £122.51/m².'

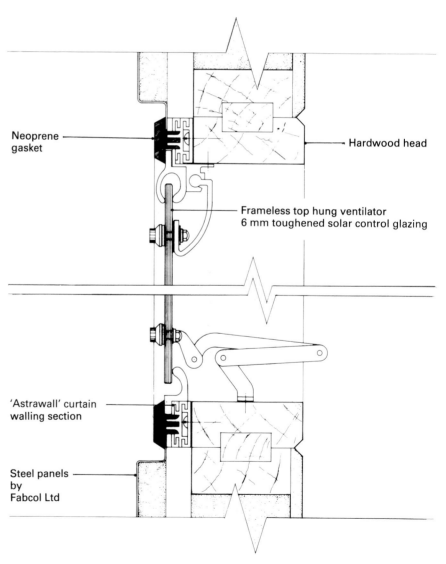

Neoprene gasket

Hardwood head

Frameless top hung ventilator
6 mm toughened solar control glazing

'Astrawall' curtain walling section

Steel panels by Fabcol Ltd

Fig. 25.2 Cross-section through ventilator by 'Astrawall'

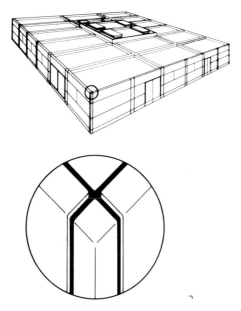

Fig. 25.3 Diagram of cladding at a corner and module junction

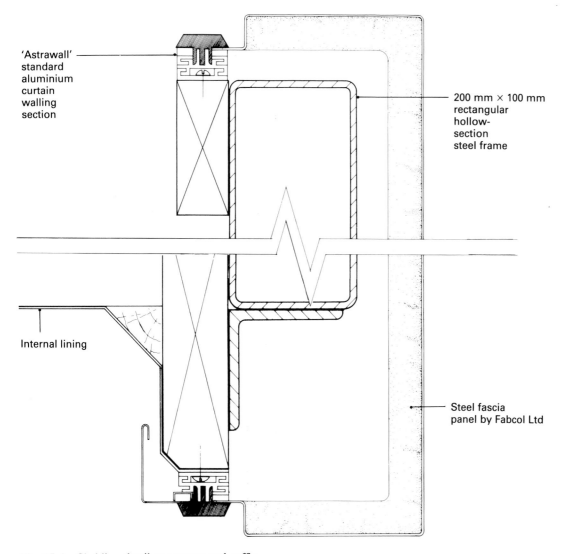

'Astrawall' standard aluminium curtain walling section

200 mm × 100 mm rectangular hollow-section steel frame

Internal lining

Steel fascia panel by Fabcol Ltd

Fig. 25.4 Cladding detail at parapet and soffit

Further reading

1. Anon (1981)
    'From Middle East to East End', *Architectural Review*, Apr. 1981, 215–16

2. Richards, C (1981)
    'South Poplar Health Centre London E14', *Architects' Journal*, 18 Feb. 1981, 299–311

3. Williams, A (1981)
    'Health and efficiency', *Building*, 10 Apr. 1981. (This very useful building dossier includes assembly drawings of the external wall and partitions — scale 1:10)

Case Study 26 Thames Water Authority, New Operations and Visitors' Centre, Fobney

Fig. 26.1 Main entrance to Visitors' Centre (Courtesy of Richard Bryant)

General

This building, designed by architects Terry Farrell Partnership in 1982, is situated on the bank of the River Kennet at Fobney, near Reading. The H-shaped plan was determined by two main factors. Firstly, for planning reasons, the building is split into three main areas with the cross gallery of the visitors' centre connecting the offices and laboratories to the operation areas. Secondly, the building rests on top of a monolithic tank structure which is sunk 5 m into the ground and determines the overall plan shape of the structure above.

Cladding

The planners required the exterior of the building to relate to the landscape and the client wanted a low-maintenance exterior. The result is a 'Presslock'

131

aluminium curtain wall, by Modern Art Glass, similar to that used at Chester-le-Street and Winwick Quay 4 (see case studies 5 and 30) supporting light blue opaque panels, which reflect the colour of the sky. These are formed by 6-mm toughened glass with epoxy pigment fused to the back side of the panel and fixed using the standard 'Presslock' neoprene gasket. One of the important features of the building is the curving façade symbolising the flow of water over the building form. These curved panels are formed in 6-mm curved clear glass with reflective film on the inside face to reduce heat gain and to help bond glass in case of breakage. Cost of the external wall and windows is given as £159.62/m² in 1982.

On the southern elevation, perforated louvres have been fixed to the vertical part of the external wall but no protection is provided to the curved glass above. The 10-mm diameter perforations in 3-mm curved aluminium louvres are designed to eliminate direct sunlight but allow diffused light to enter the rooms and thus reduce glare caused by contrast between the clear glazing and the opaque louvre blades.

Roofing

The flat roof between the curved glazing is formed using 100-mm steel decking spanning 5 m between steelwork, supporting 1.5-mm PVC roofing membrane over 35-mm insulation.

Interior

Although the outside appearance of the building is relatively sophisticated, the internal quality of detailing has some shortcomings, possibly reflecting the money available for interior finishes and fittings within a total budget. However, the rather 'stage set' interior thus presented may be appropriate for the function of Fobney as a visitors' centre and the sense of 'thinness' of detail may reflect a real desire by the architect for an illusion of space.

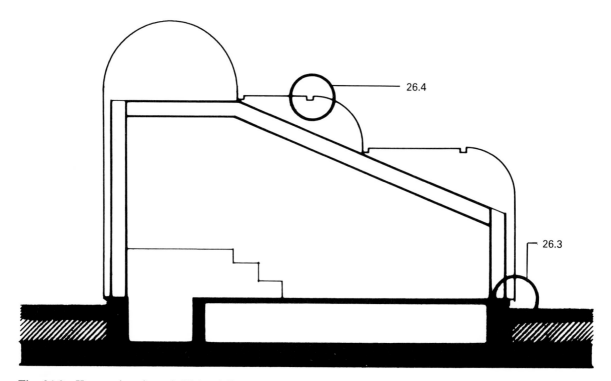

Fig. 26.2 Key section through Visitors' Centre

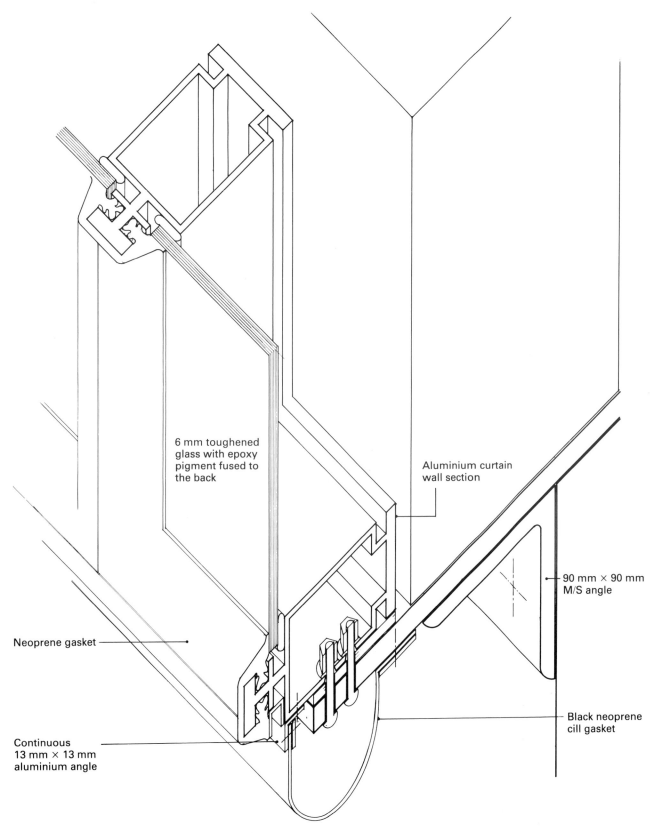

6 mm toughened glass with epoxy pigment fused to the back

Aluminium curtain wall section

90 mm × 90 mm M/S angle

Neoprene gasket

Black neoprene cill gasket

Continuous 13 mm × 13 mm aluminium angle

Fig. 26.3 Detail at cill condition (Courtesy of Eric Ng)

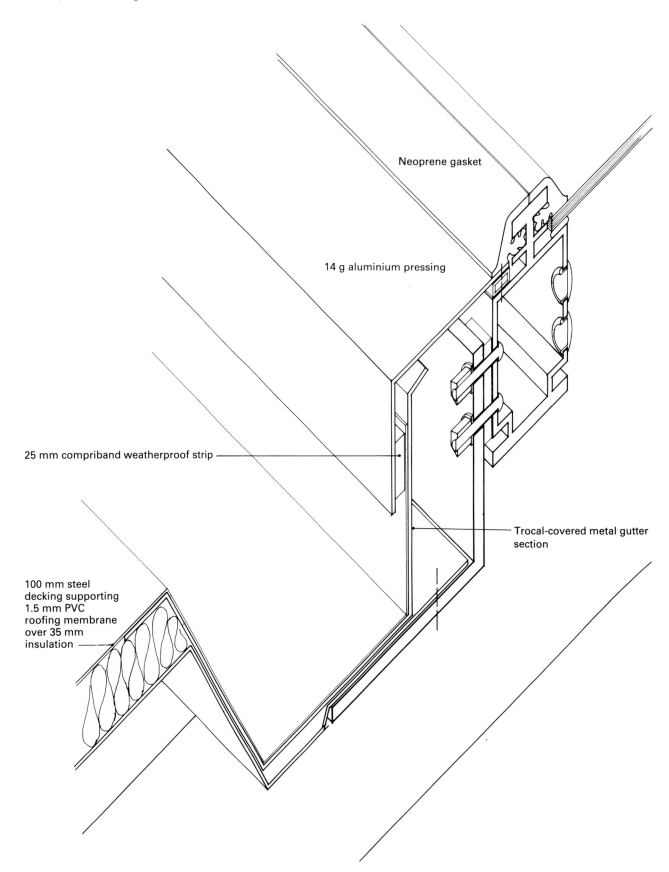

Neoprene gasket

14 g aluminium pressing

25 mm compriband weatherproof strip

Trocal-covered metal gutter section

100 mm steel decking supporting 1.5 mm PVC roofing membrane over 35 mm insulation

Fig. 26.4 Detail at eaves condition showing profiled roof meeting curtain walling

Fig. 26.5 Interior view showing glazing bars (Photo by Sarah Foster)

Fig. 26.6 Detail of glazing bars

Further reading

1. Hannay, P & Poole, D (1982)
   'Building study: Farrell at Fobney', *Architects' Journal*, 10 Nov. 1982, 67–82

2. Papadakis, A (1982)
   British Architecture. Academy Editions, London, 1982

Case Study 27 UOP Fragrances Factory, Tadworth, Surrey

Fig. 27.1 Elevation of building showing hole in the wall windows (Courtesy of Brecht-Einzig Ltd)

General

Designed by Richard Rogers and Partners and completed in 1974, this building is well known for its early use of large glass-reinforced cement (GRC) cladding panels. The single-storey building, 1580 m², accommodates administration, laboratories and stores. Speed of construction, a high resale value and minimum capital and maintenance cost, as well as a pleasant working environment, were key factors in the brief.

Cladding

The panels, supplied by Elkalite Ltd, are 5.18 m high by 2.43 m wide. Solid panels weigh 1 tonne and span 4 m between concrete floor slab and steel lattice roof edge beam. The panels were formed by 130 mm of expanded polystyrene sandwiched between two skins of GRC each 10 mm thick. Total thickness of panel was thus 150 mm. The sandwich panels were stiffened by making webs between GRC skins to create an egg-box construction encapsulating the expanded polystyrene blocks. As a result, there was some ghosting or pattern staining on the panel face, which was accentuated when a urethane coating was applied on site.

Final finish was achieved using a sealer and two finishing coats of urethane-based system which were applied on site by a roller to produce a semi-gloss, originally lime green colour, impermeable finish outside. The use of such an impermeable paint finish is no longer recommended, as it does not allow the GRC to breathe.

The panels were located on a 125 mm by 75 mm by 12.5 mm cill angle by small nibs in the base of each panel. Top restraint was achieved with mild steel T-cramps, bedded with polysulphide into location slots on the panel edge and bolted to cleats at the top and bottom of the primary steel-work edge beam.

Jointing

The 25-mm joints between panels were sealed by neoprene push-fit 'fir cone' extrusions by Hertfordshire Polymer Products Ltd. These 'fir cone' gaskets, incorporating barbed legs, can be pushed into any position including the corner panels. They do, however, depend upon extremely tight tolerances and accurate panel location, which was achieved by the use of the slotted holes and T-cramps. Good quality of the edge profile, possibly using marine-ply moulds, was also necessary for this type of push-fit gasket. The cavity within the joint assembly was used as an electrical cable route.

Windows

Opening aluminium windows by Essex Aluminium, Southminster were fixed directly into openings in the panels and sealed with neoprene compression gaskets. Fixed windows using 6-mm float glass were zipped into the moulded nib of the GRC panels. Glazed panels weigh 850 kg.

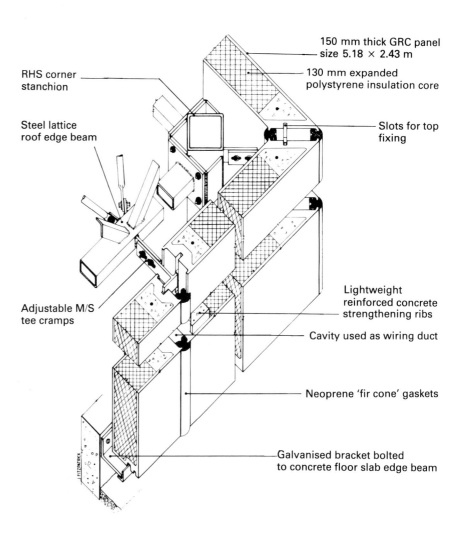

RHS corner stanchion

Steel lattice roof edge beam

Adjustable M/S tee cramps

150 mm thick GRC panel size 5.18 × 2.43 m

130 mm expanded polystyrene insulation core

Slots for top fixing

Lightweight reinforced concrete strengthening ribs

Cavity used as wiring duct

Neoprene 'fir cone' gaskets

Galvanised bracket bolted to concrete floor slab edge beam

Fig. 27.2 Assembly of GRC panels with gasket joint (Courtesy of J. Fitzpatrick)

Further reading

1. Brookes, A J & Ward, M (1981)
    'The art of construction — GRC claddings', *Architectural Journal*, 15
    July 1981, 133

2. Rabeneck, A (1974)
    'Factory, Tadworth, Surrey', *Architectural Review*, No. 934, Dec. 1974,
    337–45

3. Young, J (1980)
    Designing with GRC — Case Study 1. Architectural Press, London,
    1980, pp. 7–8

Case Study 28 Water Research Centre, Swindon

Fig. 28.1 Corner view of GRP panels

General

The Water Research Centre built in 1981 includes office space for research engineers, laboratories dealing with electrical and general materials, an experimental test hall for engineering and communal facilities, including administration, computer, library, filing, meeting and coffee areas and reception. The building is arranged as two blocks of laboratory accommodation with a continuous circulation spine in the split between them accommodating all ancillary spaces and services distribution. In addition, the client required the ability to adapt and rearrange working areas to accommodate changing research programmes and that the Centre should reflect an image of 'expertise in engineering'.

The solution adopted by the architects (Architects Design Partnership) to enable ease of adaptation and expansion was of a component cladding system hung on a steel frame. Although this bright blue cladding system has the appearance of a pressed-metal panel system with exposed fixings, it is in fact manufactured from GRP.

The structure is simply a column and beam system, with the circular hollow-section columns located externally to maximise the usable floor area. Originally, this structure was designed to be fire protected by water filling but the final solution adopted concrete filling, reinforced conventionally. The columns were site painted in a bright red colour.

Wall panels

The GRP panels consist of 3-mm outer skin with 40-mm expanded poly-urethane-foam insulation bonded to inner panel and with 34 mm by 44 mm softwood framing and blocks at fixing positions. The smooth inner skin is finished with off-white colour. The exterior colour is blue with a red colour finish on recessed horizontal fixing bands. Panels are fixed to the steel angles at top and bottom using self-drilling bolts with neoprene seal caps. The joints are 10-mm bitumen-impregnated compressible foam with silicone sealant, coloured black outside and grey inside.

The GRP panels incorporate a 0.9-mm mild steel strip encapsulated in the laminate at the edges of the panel to stiffen the panel sides.

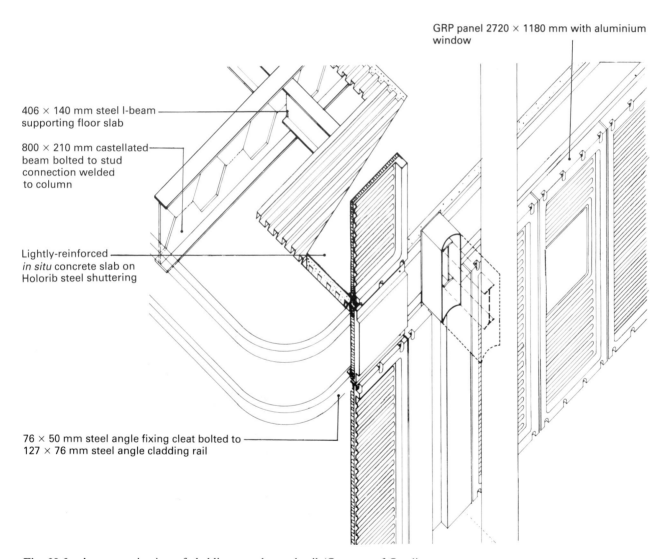

GRP panel 2720 × 1180 mm with aluminium window

406 × 140 mm steel I-beam supporting floor slab

800 × 210 mm castellated beam bolted to stud connection welded to column

Lightly-reinforced *in situ* concrete slab on Holorib steel shuttering

76 × 50 mm steel angle fixing cleat bolted to 127 × 76 mm steel angle cladding rail

Fig. 28.2 Axonometric view of cladding to column detail (Courtesy of Caroline West)

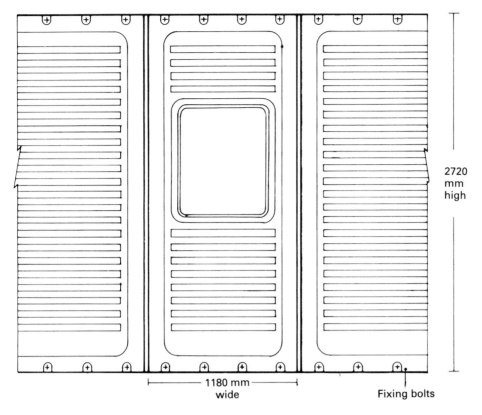

Fig. 28.3 Elevation of panels

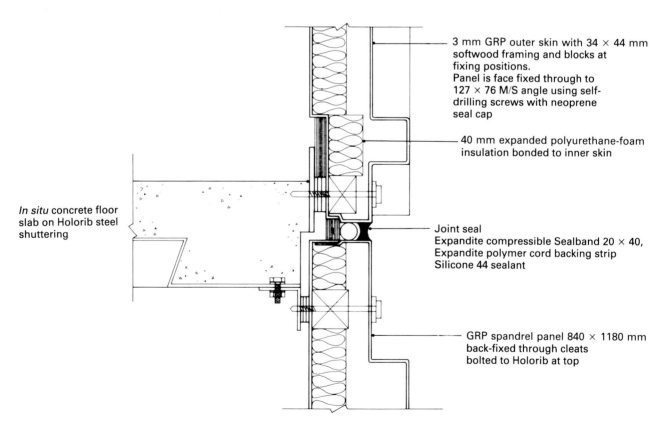

3 mm GRP outer skin with 34 × 44 mm softwood framing and blocks at fixing positions.
Panel is face fixed through to 127 × 76 M/S angle using self-drilling screws with neoprene seal cap

40 mm expanded polyurethane-foam insulation bonded to inner skin

In situ concrete floor slab on Holorib steel shuttering

Joint seal
Expandite compressible Sealband 20 × 40,
Expandite polymer cord backing strip
Silicone 44 sealant

GRP spandrel panel 840 × 1180 mm back-fixed through cleats bolted to Holorib at top

Fig. 28.4 Horizontal joint between panels

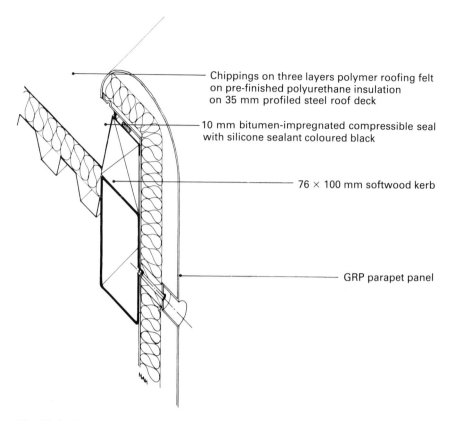

Chippings on three layers polymer roofing felt
on pre-finished polyurethane insulation
on 35 mm profiled steel roof deck

10 mm bitumen-impregnated compressible seal
with silicone sealant coloured black

76 × 100 mm softwood kerb

GRP parapet panel

Fig. 28.5 Parapet detail

Further reading

1. Deeming, N (1983)
    'Fire safe structural steel — case study Water Research Centre, Swindon', pp. 94–102. B.Arch. Dissertation, Liverpool University School of Architecture, 1983

2. Richard, O (1982)
    'Building study on Engineering Research Centre Swindon', *Architects' Journal*, 24 Feb. 1982

Case Study 29　Willis Faber and Dumas Insurance Building, Ipswich

Fig. 29.1　Reflective glass wall around the perimeter of the building

General

This building, designed by Foster Associates in 1974, set out to create an efficient working environment for 1300 people and provide 21 000 ft² of floor space on a site in the centre of Ipswich, sensitive to the scale of a market town. This has been achieved by using a reflective glass wall around the complete perimeter of the site. Inside, moving escalators rise through a top-lit space to the office areas with roof garden above.

Structure

The structure is composed of three floors of waffle slabs supported on circular columns in a 14 m by 14 m grid. The edge cantilever spans between perimeter columns at 7-m centres.

Glass wall assembly

The glass wall was specially designed and developed by Pilkington Brothers and Foster Associates, who took the Pilkington suspended glass-wall system and adapted it to solve the problem of building shape, tolerances and movement. The 930 panels of 2 m by 2.5 m specially toughened 12-mm thick bronze-tinted 'Antisun' solar control glass are hung from the roof and the suspended access floors. The glass panels, which are connected together with brass patch fittings, are literally suspended at the top panel by one central bolt, the load being spread across the width of glass by means of a top clamping strip. Lateral restraint against wind loads is provided by half-storey height glass fins, which are independently bolted to the concrete structure with metal angles.

The problem of movement and differential thermal expansion between the glass façade and the building is overcome firstly by the sliding patch connectors at the glass panel to fin junctions and, secondly, by the channel cast into the concrete slab at the base of the assembly. In this way, bottoming of the glass edges is prevented and the façade always remains in a suspended state.

Method of securing glass plates together

At each floor and at mid-floor levels, brass patch fittings connect the glass plates together and connect them back to the glass stiffening fins. The patch plates have been designed to ensure:

(a) Removal of maximum stress areas from around the holes in each glass plate.
(b) Moderation of the clamping forces necessary to avoid high peripheral stress.

The fixing bolts clamping the patch fittings together through the glass plates are in stainless steel. Patch fittings at right angles to the façade connect with the glass fins. I have previously reported on the development of this detail in Chapter 6 of *Cladding of Buildings*. Joints between the glass plates are sealed with translucent silicone sealant. The whole system was designed to accommodate errors in the concrete frame of 50 mm in any direction and was assembled by Modern Art Glass Company Limited.

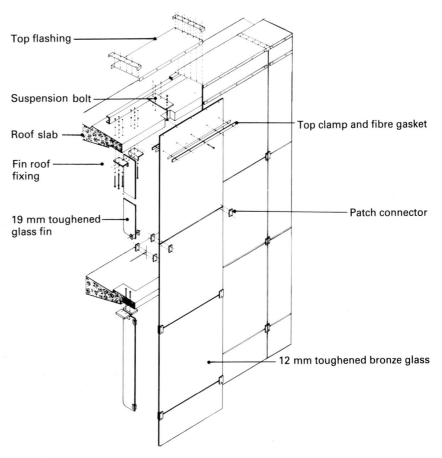

Fig. 29.2 Exploded view showing typical parts of glass wall assembly

145

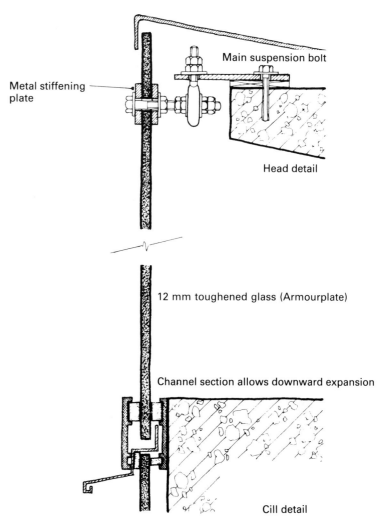

Fig. 29.3 Method of fixing using metal stiffening plate

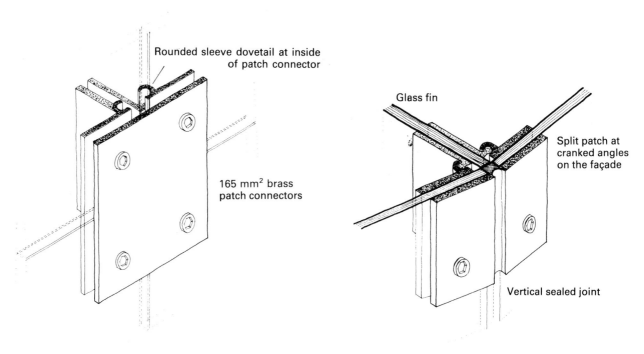

Fig. 29.4 Detail of patch connectors

Further reading

References to the details in trade information and journals show conflicting information on the design of the assembly and, for this reason, I have included comment on each source. These are:

Architectural Design, Vol. 42, No. 11, Nov. 1972, 686–701
An account of the development of the architect's brief and design solution.

Architectural Design, Vol. 45, No. 7, July 1975, 418–19
A two-page brief description of the building with small-scale plans and sections. Includes a short passage on structure and glazing systems. This information is very useful. Its content is similar to that occurring in *Architectural Design*, Vol. 47, 1977, and *Architectural Review*, Vol. 158, Sept. 1975.

Architectural Design, Vol. 47, No.9–10, 1977
Explains Norman Foster's design philosophy for the building. Includes a brief description of how the glass curtain wall performs. An exploded isometric detail showing how the glass curtain wall is suspended is very useful. A similar drawing is shown in *Architectural Review*, Vol. 158, Sept. 1975, but here the scale is slightly larger and therefore clearer. An isometric is shown of a patch fitting which is incorrect. It would not resist any horizontal movement. The correct version is shown in both *Architectural Review*, Vol. 158, Sept. 1975, and *Design*, No. 321, Sept. 1975, where the rounded locating nib resists the horizontal movement.

Architects' Journal, Vol. 161, No. 23, 4 June 1975, 1160–2
A two-page preview to a full review in *Architectural Review*, Sept. 1975, includes photographs and a short description of little use.

Architectural Review, Vol. 158, Sept. 1975, 130–54
A complete building review from design concepts through to structural and glazing details. The glazing is explained clearly, although the exploded isometric of the glass wall assembly is of a small scale and difficult to read and understand. A larger-scale detail is included in *Architectural Design*, Vol. 47, which is easier to read. A section is also shown through the whole wall and an isometric shows the correct form of patch plate.

Design, No. 321, Sept. 1975, 42–9
A collection of photographs and drawings with short description of each. The details shown for the glazing wall are useful but only partly explain how the glazing system works. Detail of the glass suspension points shown differs from the detail shown on the exploded isometric drawings. This is the only article which shows the glazing detail at floorline.

RIBA Journal, Vol. 84, No. 8, Aug. 1977, 330–54
Award details only.

Pilkington Design Guide for Armourplate suspended glass assemblies gives the design data and requirements for general installation. Also gives reasons behind the design solutions.

Banham, R *Foster Associates*. RIBA Publications Ltd, 1979, pp. 46–7
Short description and photographs of the building only.

Case Study 30   Winwick Quay 4 and 7, Industrial Units, Warrington

Fig. 30.1   Elevation of Unit 4 composed of interchangeable solid panels, glazing or louvres

General

This award-winning scheme was designed by architects Farrell and Grimshaw Partnership in 1980 and includes 7648 m² floor area for warehouse space, industrial areas or offices to let by a number of individual tenants. The client, Warrington Development Corporation, requested the architects to investigate a more flexible and adaptable scheme for the provision of industrial floorspace. As such, it has some similarity with the Herman Miller Factory at Bath by the same architects (see case study 11) in that the cladding is made up from a system of either solid panels, glazing or louvres, which are interchangeable within a 'Presslock' gasketing system.

The scheme is based upon a structural grid of 10 m by 17.5 m bays with primary beams at 10-m centres. There are no secondary beams and the roof deck is made up from deep profiled Plannja 200 roof decking which span continuously over the primary beams. The decking was designed to deflect to provide internal roof drainage but problems of bird feathers (the site had been a rubbish disposal area) caused internal gutters to block and a subsequent build-up of water caused part of the roof to collapse. In order to prevent this recurring, drain holes have now been incorporated in the parapet panels with subsequent staining of the panel surface (see Fig 30.1).

Cladding

The cladding subframe, comprising 150 mm by 23 mm 'Presslock' aluminium carrier system, developed by Modern Art Glass Limited, spans 4.8 m between a power-floated concrete floor slab and a lattice truss which runs at eaves level around the perimeter. These vertical mullions are spaced at 1.25-m centres with smaller 125 mm by 23 mm aluminium transoms between the mullions at floor and intermediate levels. Smaller transoms (nosing sections) were used for curved corners and eaves.

'Alucobond' panels, 2.4 m by 1.25 m, are then mounted on to the aluminium carrier system using neoprene gaskets. These panels with an anodic silver finish form the main opaque cladding unit. 'Alucobond', manufactured by Anglo Swiss Aluminium Limited, who import the material as flat sheets, consists of two sheets of aluminium (Peralumen NS 41) each 0.5 mm thick, bonded to a low-density polyethylene core, bringing the overall thickness to 6 mm. These are then interchangeable with 6-mm float glass. The top curved 'Alucobond' was formed by Mott Aluminium Company Limited. At the corners of the building, the fascia panels were produced in GRP and painted to match the 'Alucobond'. This was because the 'Alucobond' cannot be curved in two directions.

Farrell and Grimshaw designed the building with a high level of roof insulation. Thus, although the cladding panels are not insulated, the building still satisfied the thermal performance requirements of the Building Regulations part FF. Any further insulation of the walls is left to the responsibility of the individual tenants. This system of 'Presslock' curtain walling and 'Alucobond' was also used later at Chester-le-Street Civic Centre (see case study 5) where it can be seen that it was developed to include an insulation core and inner lining.

All three types of cladding panel — opaque, glazed and louvres — are held into their subframes by a push-fit, preformed, continuous neoprene gasket. At the base of the building, an extruded neoprene tolerance strip is used between the lower aluminium cladding transom and concrete slab. It is tucked into the transom and screwed to a pressed-aluminium cill, which is in turn screwed to the concrete floor slab. This detail was also used at Chester-le-Street.

Because of the need to bring services into the building at any point, the 'Alucobond' panels were cut to receive silver-finished GRP service hoods, which were fixed into the 'Alucobond' with an H-section zipper gasket.

Winwick Quay 7

On the same site and immediately opposite Winwick Quay 4 is Unit 7, designed by Nicholas Grimshaw Partnership in 1982. Here the cladding is composed of steel-faced composite panels by Hoesch, fitting on to a steel frame with GRP curved leaves detail, similar to that used at the IBM Sports Centre (see case study 15). This building also deserves further investigation by the reader and the detail of the external wall is included here for that reason.

Here, the Hoesch LL100 panels, 100 mm thick, 1000 mm high, span 5 m without any additional secondary steelwork (cost quoted by Williams[4] as £32.34 per m², which seems remarkably low) separated by the twin-skin GRP eaves and corner panels by Anmac Limited, which introduces diffused lighting into the production and office spaces.

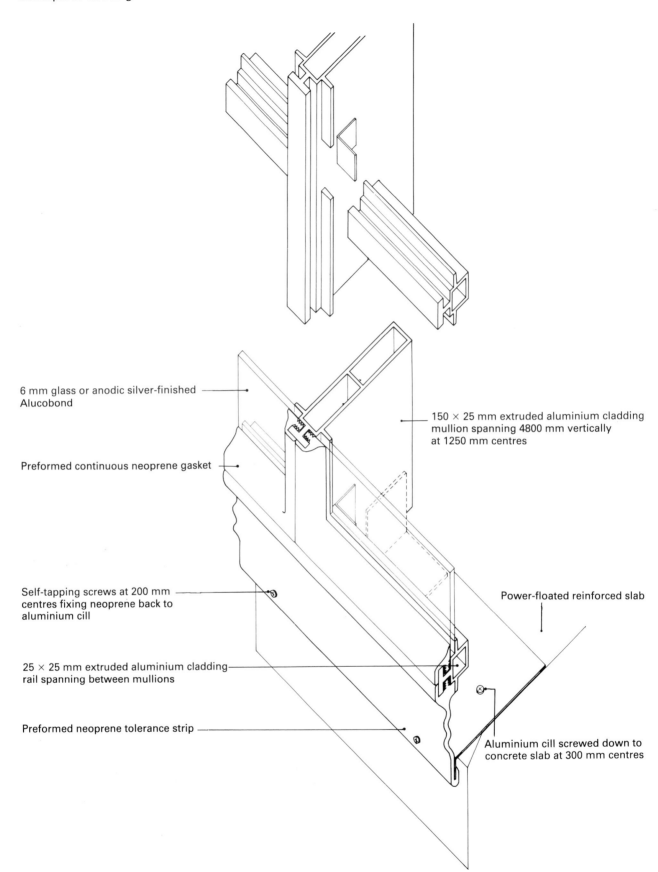

6 mm glass or anodic silver-finished Alucobond

150 × 25 mm extruded aluminium cladding mullion spanning 4800 mm vertically at 1250 mm centres

Preformed continuous neoprene gasket

Self-tapping screws at 200 mm centres fixing neoprene back to aluminium cill

Power-floated reinforced slab

25 × 25 mm extruded aluminium cladding rail spanning between mullions

Preformed neoprene tolerance strip

Aluminium cill screwed down to concrete slab at 300 mm centres

Fig. 30.2   Unit 4 — cill detail to edge of slab

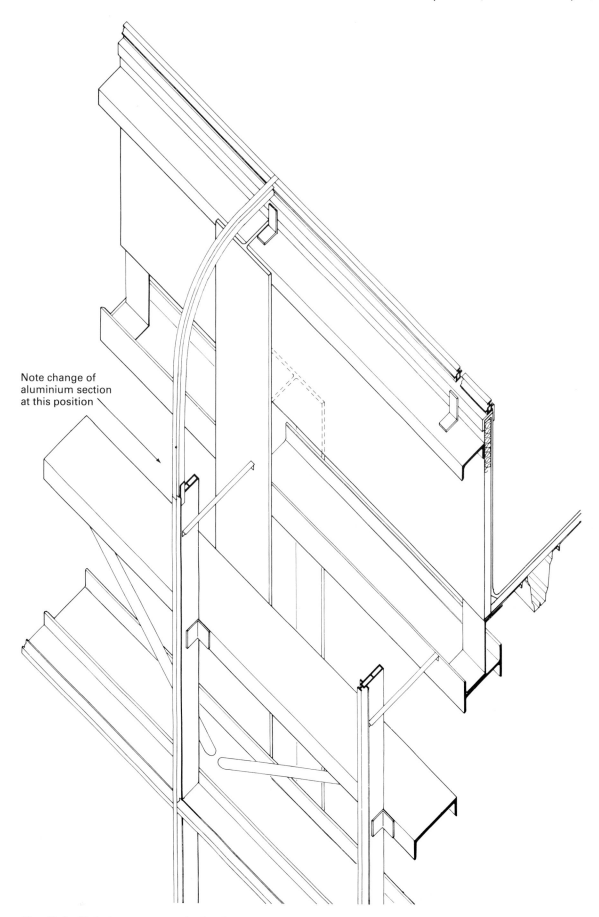

Note change of
aluminium section
at this position

Fig. 30.3 Unit 4 — axonometric showing construction of vertical mullions at
eaves level (Courtesy of G. Heywood)

Fig. 30.4 Corner of Unit 4 showing GRP fascia panel

Fig. 30.5 Typical bay with exposed neoprene gaskets around panel (note leaching)

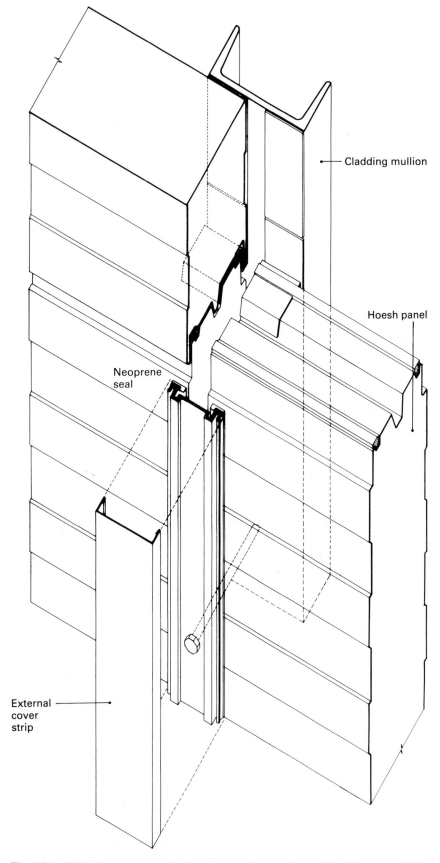

Cladding mullion

Hoesh panel

Neoprene seal

External cover strip

Fig. 30.6 Unit 7 — axonometric showing panel to panel assembly (Courtesy of Hin Tan)

Fig. 30.7 Unit 7 — view of loading bay

Fig. 30.8 Unit 7 — close-up of panel showing horizontal profile of Hoesch panel

Further reading

1. Brookes, A J (1980)
   'Products in practice — Claddings 2', *Architects' Journal*, 5 Nov. 1980, 910

2. Brookes, A J & Ward, M (1981)
   'The art of construction — metal claddings, part 2 case studies', *Architects' Journal*, 15 July 1981, 124–5

3. Murray, P (1980)
   'Design for change', *RIBA Journal*, Vol. 87, Jan. 1980, 31–6

4. Williams, A (1983)
   'Winwick Quay 7 — building dossier', *Building*, 28 Oct. 1983

Index

Acorn Anodising 51
Advanced Factory Units, Milton Keynes 81–6
Alphire 91
Alucobond 20, 21, 149
Aluflex 45
Aluminium Systems, Dublin 48, 114
Aluzinc 4
Anglo Swiss Aluminium, Ltd 149
Anmac, Ltd 149
Anthony Hunt Associates 41
Antisun Glass 73
Arbokol 13
Architects Design Partnership 140
Armourplate glass 101, 108
Arne Jacobsen, Dissing and Weitling 29
Artech Plastics 47
Arup Associates 16, 18, 32
Astrawall 128
Aztec West 1–7, 115

Bayer (UK) Ltd 26
Becker and Becker and Partner 56
Benson Electrics 4, 6, 7
Bespak Factory 8–11, 125
Botschi, P. 70
Botta, M. 121
Brett, P. 4
Brian Taggart Associates 4, 6
Briggs Amasco 124
British Aluminium Co. Ltd 32, 114
Brock Carmichael Associates 124
Buildex 101
Burne House Telecommunications Centre 12–15, 87
Bush Lane House 16–19

Cambridge Design 8
Chagnas Construction Metallique 38
Charles Pearson, Son and Partners 12
Chester-Le-Street Civic Centre 20–4, 57, 133, 149
Climax Building Gaskets 91
Colonnades Garden Centre 25–8
Compriband 21
Crawford Door Ltd 1–7, 45, 65
Crittall Construction 12

Dale, Nigel 90
Danish Embassy 29–31
Department of Health 127
Derek Stowe and Partners 127

Elkalite, Ltd 137
Escol Panels 12, 61, 87
Essex Aluminium, Southminster 7, 138
Enternit 10
Ethafoam 88

F J Samuely and Partners 64
Fabcol, Ltd 128, 129
Farrell Grimshaw Partnership 47, 148, 149
Faulkner-Brown Hendy Watkinson Stoner 20
Festival Hall, Liverpool 26, 32–6
Fir Cone Gaskets 4, 5, 65, 138
Fishtails 76, 78, 79
Fleetguard Factory 37–40
Fobney 131
Forster Steel 91
Foster Associates vii, 7, 100, 114, 144

Glass Reinforced Cement (GRC) 137–8
Glass Reinforced Plastic (GRP) 47–9, 65, 140–3, 149, 152
Gowan James 120
Greene King Brewery 38, 41–6

Herman Miller Factory, Bath viii, 1, 47–50, 57, 148
Herman Miller Warehouse, Chippenham 51–5
Hertfordshire Polymer Products, Ltd 138
Heywood Williams 125
Hochhaus Dresdner Bank 56–60
Hoesch Panels 149, 153
Hopkins, Michael: Architects 90
Hunt, Anthony Associates 91

IBM Midlands Marketing Centre 61–3
IBM Sports Hall 64–8
Inmos Microchip Factory viii, 69–73, 87

John Gaytten Associates 87
Jon Windows Ltd 70
Jordans of Bristol 76
Josef Gartner, Ltd 56, 76

Kaplicky, Jan vii
Kinain Workshops 51

Leyland and Birmingham Rubber Co viii, 48, 114, 115
Lloyds Redevelopment 75–80
Longton Industrial Holdings 90

Makrolon 33
Merseyside Development Corporation 32
Michael Hopkins Architects vii, 41, 90
Milton Keynes Development Corporation 81
Modern Art Glass 20, 48, 114, 115, 133, 145, 149
Mott Aluminium Co. Ltd 149

Nicholas Grimshaw and Partners 1, 51, 149
Norweb Offices, Ashton-under-Lyne 87–9

Oil Canning 91
Ove Arup and Partners 16, 37, 100

Patch Fittings 145, 146
Patera System 64, 90–8
Peter Brett Associates 4, 51
Peralumen 149
Phenelux 115
Pilkington Bros. 101, 144
Planar Glazing System 101, 107
Plannja Dobel Ltd 38, 41, 42, 44, 64, 148
Plastisol 124
Polycarbonate Sheeting 26–8, 33–6
Polyester Powder Coat 7, 52, 128
Pritchard, Tony 114
Presslock 21, 22, 131, 148
Prouvé, J. vii, 81
PVF^2 37, 38, 41, 70, 101

Renault Factory 38, 73, 100–13
Richard Rogers and Partners vii, 37, 69, 75, 137
R M Douglas 51

Rockwool Insulation 38, 39, 52, 78
R.V.P. Building Products, Ltd 101

Sainsbury Centre 7, 114–19
Schreiber Factory 124–6
Schreiber House 120–3
Silicone Jointing 61, 65, 141, 145
South Poplar Health Centre 127–130
Stelvetite 81
Stainless Steel 76–9
Styrofoam 7
Supalux 125
Superform Metals 4, 114, 117
Synthapulvin 51, 52, 128

Terry Farrell Partnership 25, 26
Thames Water Authority New Operations Centre 131–6
Tubeworkers, Ltd 69

Unistrut 51–3
University of East Anglia 114
U.O.P. Fragrance Factory 137–9

Vacuum Forming 4
Vitreous Enamelling 13–15, 61–3, 87–9

Warrington Development Corporation 148
Water Research Centre 140–3
Water Cooled Columns 16–19
Whitby, Mark 91
Willis Faber and Dumas 101, 144–7
Winwick Quay 1, 20, 65, 133, 148–54

Yorke, Rosenburg and Mardall 61
Young, J. 70

Zipper Gasket 128